Beyond Ashes

Beyond Ashes

A TRUE STORY
OF SURVIVAL
AND TRIUMPH

MARLYN OLSEN VISTAUNET

with PHYLLIS GEORGE MCFARLAND

Nampa, Idaho | Oshawa, Ontario, Canada
www.pacificpress.com

Cover design by Steve Lanto
Cover design resources from iStockphoto.com
Inside design by Aaron Troia

Copyright © 2018 by Pacific Press® Publishing Association
Printed in the United States of America
All rights reserved

The author assumes full responsibility for the accuracy of all facts and quotations as cited in this book.

Some names and places have been changed to protect privacy.

Scripture quotations marked KJV are from the King James Version.

Scripture quotations marked NIV® are from THE HOLY BIBLE, NEW INTERNATIONAL VERSION®. Copyright © 1973, 1978, 1984, 2011 by Biblica, Inc.® Used by permission. All rights reserved worldwide.

Scripture marked NKJV is taken from the New King James Version®. Copyright © 1982 by Thomas Nelson. Used by permission. All rights reserved.

Scripture quotations marked NLT are taken from the Holy Bible, New Living Translation, copyright © 1996, 2004, 2007, 2013, 2015 by Tyndale House Foundation. Used by permission of Tyndale House Publishers, Inc., Carol Stream, Illinois 60188. All rights reserved.

Additional copies of this book can be purchased by calling toll-free 1-800-765-6955 or by visiting AdventistBookCenter.com.

ISBN 978-0-8163-6373-5

March 2018

Dedication

This book is dedicated to my loving children, Laura, Ernie, and Tamara. Thank you for giving me the sweetest gifts in my life—my grandchildren, Justin, Brittany (Travis), Joshua (Mercedie), Jared (Jessie), Tanner, Paul, and Genie. Your energy, devotion, and enthusiasm keep me centered and bring incredible joy in my journey. I love you to the moon and beyond!

Contents

Preface	O Love That Will Not Let Me Go	9
Acknowledgments		13
Introduction		15
Chapter 1	Little Girl Lost	17
Chapter 2	California, Here We Come!	27
Chapter 3	Seven Is the Perfect Number	37
Chapter 4	New Places, New Faces	43
Chapter 5	"Mrs. Cardoza, I Want to Take You With Me"	51
Chapter 6	"Marlyn, Don't Be Afraid"	57
Chapter 7	Torch on the Hill	65
Chapter 8	Could I Be in the Wrong Room?	71
Chapter 9	Would Spring Ever Come Again?	77
Chapter 10	Homecoming!	83
Chapter 11	"I Don't Know What Else It Could Have Been!"	89
Chapter 12	We Were So Lucky!	95
Chapter 13	Look Out, Lodi—Here I Come!	101
Chapter 14	Kaleidoscope of Fun and Fanfare	109
Chapter 15	Finding True Love or Something Like That	115
Chapter 16	Tossed Out and Nowhere to Go	121
Chapter 17	City Jungle	127
Chapter 18	Three Surprise Visits	131
Chapter 19	Four Close Calls	137
Chapter 20	I'm That Girl	145
Chapter 21	"Daddy, Wake Up!"	151

Chapter 22	A Turn in the Road	157
Chapter 23	War Comes Home	163
Chapter 24	The Light Shines in the Darkness	169
Chapter 25	When God Writes Your Love Story	177
Epilogue	He Restores My Soul	185

Preface

O Love That Will Not Let Me Go

lack ice. "An angel's got to stop this car!" I shrieked as the car slid downhill on a winding mountain road. The car came to a sliding stop on the edge of a precipice. On the passenger's side, my daughter, Lori, gasped as she looked down the steep rim of the icy cliff. The words of the song on the radio, "O Love That Will Not Let Me Go," penetrated our thumping hearts. We silently bowed our heads in thankfulness for God's care.

Isn't that what life is like? Often we find ourselves on the edge of a precipice—danger, illness, death, conflict, failure, sorrow, unfair circumstances, and on and on the list goes. As Christians, we have the spiritual DNA of the Almighty God, who is the Author and Finisher of our faith. Embracing His love through difficult times is the key to knowing and loving Him.

David the psalmist wrote the most incredible collection of songs and prayers ever. In these prayers, he freely shared his emotions with God—love, joy, praise, exuberance, compassion, anger, defeat, grief, anguish, depression, *crippling fear*—emotions with which I could identify. It was in times like these that I began honestly to give God the raw feelings of my heart. I would miraculously be ushered into the presence of a most loving and merciful God—*far beyond my expectations.*

We all have different fingerprints. We come with different backgrounds, and each of us is uniquely special. God knows and respects our uniqueness. He is tolerant of our limitations. As a young adult, I tended to think that the difficulties, pressures, and disasters I had already experienced were unfair intrusions into what should have been rightfully mine—a neat package of idealistic love and existence from a God that

Beyond Ashes

says He loves me. I at times felt awkward and out of place, as though I weren't good enough to approach Him until I proved I was a decent person—*I could not on my own.* As you've traveled your own path, perhaps you have had similar moments.

In this book, I will share the first thirty-two years of my life—stories that reveal a divine presence that have led me to the faith I now have. While some stories may seem incredible, all of them are true.

When you come to the end of the book, it does not end my story. In reality, those first thirty-two years only set the stage for the rest of my life. As you follow the journey, no matter what season of life you are in, may you reflect and marvel at how miraculously God is weaving a thread of love in your own life. With God, your story—and my story—*will* end in triumph.

It is my prayer that this book will serve as an inspiration to usher you into the presence of a loving and merciful God who will turn your ashes into beauty with a love that will not let you go. But before you turn the page, I must tell you about the world into which I was born. Yes, I was lucky I had incredible people in my life—a mother and father with a spiritual diary that could be titled "Fearless Pioneer Adventurers for God."

My father, Monrad E. Olsen, an immigrant from Norway, grew up on a farm. As a young lad, when he wasn't herding sheep, he was lassoing and training wild horses—later he became a rodeo champion riding bucking horses and lassoing wild steer, earning money to help support the family of eight children. God's hand was on Daddy all along. His adventurous spirit and desire to be in the Lord's work led him to give up his plan to become an attorney and to embrace what God had in mind for him—a missionary to Mexico, where he faithfully served the Lord for nineteen years. His early years as a cowboy had prepared him for traveling the trails that often entailed riding horseback on mountainous terrain, sometimes traveling for three days at a time to reach a village. At night, he would sleep on the ground.

Arriving in Mexico as a literature evangelist in 1929, he was employed in early 1932 by the Union Committee as field secretary for the Gulf Mission. That's where my mother comes in. Years before, in a dream, my father had seen a beautiful young woman wearing a pink dress and smiling at him. He awoke from the dream with the strong impression that

Preface

this was the woman God wanted him to marry. Daddy did not forget the dream, and always in the back of his mind he pondered the thought and looked forward to the day he would meet the woman of his dreams.

My mother, Ana María (Anita), was an only child born to Juan Alba and Edith Vega Alba. A descendent of the Duke of Alba in Spain—an aristocrat of his time—her father's bloodline immigrated to Mexico in the eighteenth century. As a state senator, Juan Alba often traveled with the president of Mexico as the president's personal pilot and advisor. Edith Alba owned a successful dress shop, and the family was financially comfortable. When my mother was ten years old, Mexico was overtaken by communism, and sadly, her father was captured and he disappeared out of their lives. When Grandma Edith and Mamá left their Catholic upbringing to become Seventh-day Adventists, they gave up their life of wealth to become traveling literature evangelists. With two dogs and two parrots, their entourage traveled by burro from town to town selling books and holding Bible studies.

For seven consecutive years, Grandma Edith held the title of champion colporteur in all of Mexico. When Daddy, now the colporteur director for the Gulf Mission, heard about Grandma Edith's success, he traveled to Torreón, where she and Mamá lived, to ask for her help in training colporteurs. Upon knocking on their door, there she stood—the woman of his dreams—a beautiful woman in a pink dress smiling at him. It was love at first sight, and the courtship began. They were married six months later in a house in Saltillo. Together they served the Lord.

In Guadalajara, a son, Franklin, and then a daughter, Wanda, were born. When Daddy was assigned to start the work in Mérida, Yucatán, the family relocated. A mission was formed with Daddy serving as president. While they lived in Mérida, I was born. A year later, our family transferred back to Guadalajara, where Daddy served as president of the mission. While Daddy was away on a trip, Mamá had to bear a traumatic difficulty alone—and that is where the first story begins.

—Marlyn Olsen Vistaunet

Acknowledgments

It takes a community to write a book—a heartfelt thanks to each and every one who have helped me climb this mountain.

First, to my parents, who convinced me at an early age that I should record the stories of my childhood; without that detailed information, I would not have otherwise been able to pen this book. For their love for God's Word, their unconditional love for their children, and for reminding me that my deepest treasure can be found in God's Word.

To Philip Samaan, speaker, author, and religion professor at Southern Adventist University, who after he heard me tell about my kidnapping experience in Mexico, urged me to write the story. The first condensed version was published in the *Adventist Review* in September 2007.

Thank you to Phyllis George McFarland, writer/editor, for the comradeship we shared as we collaborated together in the writing of the stories of my early childhood—especially in the detailed second version of "Little Girl Lost" (chapter 1). Her expert editing skills, perspective on the cosmos of words, sense of humor, and unwavering encouragement are forever cherished. Also, thank you to author and editor Ken McFarland, who at times looked over Phyllis's shoulder offering just the right advice.

To Camille McKenzie, author, life coach, and friend, who keenly convinced me that I indeed had a book, and that each experience should be recorded—the good, the difficult, and the painful. "Write with your readers in mind. Your experiences can benefit others." Thank you, Camille, for two years of encouragement and positive "thumbs up" until the work was completed.

To my husband, Pastor Loren, for standing by my side on this adventure, for listening to me recite stories, providing feedback, and giving me the go-ahead signal. Thank you for the comforting reassurance when the narrative was painful. My gratitude is without bounds.

Beyond Ashes

To the many beautiful people who served as role models in my growing up years; for their powerful influence in every conversation, every act of kindness, and for modeling that there is joy in the journey of life—joy that can be found in these pages.

To dear friends in my social media community who continually inspire me, encourage me, and enlighten me—whose personal notes and kind words are like sunshine peeking through the clouds. Many thanks for keeping my dream going.

Finally, and most important, to my Lord and Savior, Jesus Christ, who whispered the desire in my ear to write; who consistently comforted my heart, dried my tears, danced with joy, and guided and supported me when I felt like giving up. He is the Hero in this book!

Introduction

I first met Marlyn at Pine Hills Junior Academy in Auburn, California, where we were classmates—I was in eighth grade and she was in ninth. As a new student there, I heard the story of her family's catastrophic fire and was horrified by it. How could this beautiful, vivacious girl who was always laughing and smiling have come through such a tragedy?

Marlyn and I got to know each other better the following year as students together in the ninth- and tenth-grade classroom. It was a year neither of us will ever forget. Our teacher was a double amputee named Lloyd Funkhouser, a man full of hilarity, heart, and heaven's love. By his example, Mr. Funkhouser taught me courage; but his message for Marlyn was that no matter how great the tragedy, God can turn it into transcendent joy.

Marlyn and I attended different boarding academies and lost track of each other until years later, when she somehow found my phone number and invited me to visit her at the Village Chapel in McDonald, Tennessee, where her husband, Loren, was pastor. She jumped up to greet me as I walked in—the same beautiful, gracious person I remembered. As we visited together after church, it became clear to me that her life had been anything but easy. Yet I could see she had not been flattened by the hardships. Far from it! She made being a pastor's wife her personal ministry, as a caring counselor, director of youth ministries, prayer coordinator, Sabbath School class teacher, hostess, jail minister, and counselor volunteer—to name just a few.

After that, Marlyn and I stayed in touch. The more I learned about her story, the more amazed I was by it. When she confided that she was thinking about writing a book, I enthusiastically agreed: this was a story that needed to be told. From her miraculous rescue at the age of three

Beyond Ashes

from a child-trafficking ring; to the terrible loss of her little brother; to a series of mishaps, some of which could have proved fatal without God's interposition, I knew hers was a life that would prove to be the basis for a real page-turner. I especially wanted the world to meet her little brother, Milton, a child so in touch with God that at the age of seven, his house in flames and his skin burnt off, he could comfort his sister, saying quietly, "Marlyn, don't be afraid."

Over the space of the past two years, Marlyn and I have worked together to tell her story. I so want you to read it. I want you to meet Milton and learn courage from him; I want you to laugh with Marlyn as she shares her intimate recollection of youthful naïveté as an imaginative and incredibly curious teenager with a knack for trouble and misadventure; and I especially want you to be amazed at God's miraculous deliverance, time after time after time.

—Phyllis George McFarland

CHAPTER 1

Little Girl Lost

Dazzling sunlight danced on the courtyard walls of our home in Guadalajara, and gaudy parrots chattered overhead as I skipped into the house, where sweet cinnamon smells drifted from the kitchen. Oh yes! Mamá stood by the stove, stirring steaming rice pudding with a stick of *canela* (cinnamon). My three-year-old mouth wanted some of that right away!

"Por favor, Mamacita, ¡quiero un poco ahora!" ("Please, Mommy, I want some now!")

"No, Marlyn, this is for lunch. You'll have to wait until then."

I pouted, but not for long. Grandma Edith, her curly auburn braided hair coiled at the nape of her neck, stepped briskly into the kitchen. "I'm going to Zapopan to give a Bible study to Señora Figueroa." Grandma Edith was a Christian book evangelist and Bible worker. "She has two children about the ages of Frank [my nine-year-old brother] and Wanda [my five-year-old sister]. Do you suppose they would like to come with me and play while I am giving the Bible study?"

Before Mamá could answer, I began jumping up and down, squealing with excitement. "I want to go too, Mamacita! Please, can I go?"

Grandma Edith was willing, but Mamá hesitated. "Are you sure? I don't want her to be underfoot . . ."

"I won't bother her; I'll be good! I promise!" I pleaded.

"Well, all right," Mamá said resignedly. "Doña Triné!" she called. A moment later our nanny appeared at the kitchen door. "Can you get Marlyn ready for a trip to Zapopan? She's going with Grandma Edith. Put her pink dress on her; she looks nice in it. And get Wanda ready, because she's going too, unless she doesn't want to. And tell Frank to change into a clean outfit and comb his hair."

I was getting to go! Doña Triné took me to the bedroom Wanda and

Beyond Ashes

I shared and started getting me ready. "Stand still, Marlyn, and put your hands up over your head." I put my arms up, but I was far too excited to stand still. The dress went on, but then she had to comb my hair and secure it with a clip. "Stand still, Marlyn," she pleaded. But how could someone stand still when she was this excited?

A few minutes later, the four of us were climbing onto the bus. Somehow Grandma Edith found us three seats together on the crowded bus, and we settled ourselves in, with me nestled securely on her lap. Spreading trees and people on bicycles flew by us as the bus wound through the traffic, and in no time it was slowing down as we reached the village of Zapopan.

Mrs. Figueroa, tall and slender with a face alight with good humor, greeted us at the door to her house, her two children peering from behind her. "¡Entren, por favor!" she invited, and we walked into a room filled with enough knickknacks and pictures to keep a child engaged for hours. Her children, José and Rosita, quickly ran with the three of us children out to the courtyard to play. The four of them found plenty of things to do for fun; I, on the other hand, was considered a tagalong to be ignored, and I was too little to understand their games anyway.

No matter; that courtyard was a fascinating place. Creeping vines studded with blue flowers climbed the walls, a bed of red asters smiled shyly up at me, and a group of warblers swooped in for a landing on a piece of statuary. When I tried to catch one, though, they hastily flew off in a burst of wings. But then I spotted a section of the courtyard wall covered in blue-and-white tile work, with a fountain of water pouring from its middle. I tried to reach up and play in the waterspout, but it was too high, so I contented myself by dipping my hands in the pool at the bottom.

"Marlyn! Get out of the water!" shouted Wanda. I looked over at her unhappily. She wasn't the boss of me! But I got up anyway and wandered off in the direction of the doorway to the living room. I knew Grandma Edith was in that room full of interesting knickknacks.

"No, Marlyn, not in there! We're not supposed to bother Grandma Edith!" Now it was Frank yelling at me! Maybe I could play with the big kids. But they shooed me off and went on with their play. Disgusted, I plumped down by a small palm tree in the middle of the courtyard. This was taking too long, and I was getting hungry. Some rice pudding would

Little Girl Lost

taste pretty good right about now. The best thing to do might be to walk home and get some lunch.

I found the gate leading to the street. Its latch was very high, so I stretched up as far as I possibly could. I was just a couple of inches shy of being able to reach it. I found a stray rock lying a few feet away and shoved it next to the gate and under the latch. The next attempt succeeded! I kicked the rock away, opened the gate, and skipped out onto the street.

The next job was to find home. It hadn't taken very long to get here on the bus, so home probably was just up ahead. Coming my way down the dusty street was a teenage girl in a colorful skirt. As we met, she bent down to talk to me. "Niñita, ¿adónde vas?" ("Little girl, where are you going?") she asked.

Confident I was almost home, I replied, "Voy a casa." ("I'm going home.") I pointed straight ahead to a nearby village. The girl straightened up, gave me another smile, and went on her way.

I kept walking. That village up ahead seemed to be taking longer to get to than I thought it would. But finally, there I was. I looked up and down the street. None of the houses looked like mine, but surely the people living in them knew where my family lived. I picked a big white house, walked up to the door, and knocked.

A sweet-faced young woman opened the door. Behind her, bending to peer around her, was a most unpleasant-looking man with a thin mustache stretched across his upper lip. So I directed my request to the woman: "I'm hungry, and I want some rice pudding. Can you take me to Mamá and rice pudding?"

"Come on in, little girl. What's your name?"

"I'm Marlyn."

"Well, Marlyn, we don't have any rice pudding, but we do have some frijoles and tortillas. How does that sound?"

That sounded good to me, and soon I was happily chowing down on the frijoles and tortillas. Once I was full, I told the woman I was ready to go see Mamá. She promised to take me, but first, she said, I needed a nap. She took me into a bedroom and helped me onto the bed, and I happily settled down for a nap.

When I woke up, I again announced that I was ready to go see Mamá. The woman promised to take me soon, but not yet. *Not yet? Why not?* I

Beyond Ashes

wondered. Then I got very sleepy, and that is the last thing I remembered until late the next day.

The rest of the story unfolded when I was not around to know about it, so I will have to tell it as it was told to me.

When Grandma Edith finished the Bible study, she gathered her things and stepped into the courtyard to call the children. Wanda and Frank came running. But, *Where was Marlyn?* Wanda and Frank looked at each other blankly, dismay spreading over their faces as they realized they had not seen their sister in some time. Grandma Edith, realizing they did not know my whereabouts, became dismayed as well. Everyone, including Señora Figueroa and her two children, began looking for me everywhere—in every nook and cranny in each room of the house, double-checking the courtyard, and finally out on the street. "Marlyn! Marlyn!" they called desperately, fanning out through the streets and fields. Then Grandma Edith encountered a teenage girl walking down the street who recognized the name Marlyn right away.

"¡Señora! ¡Señora! My name is María, and I saw a little girl who called herself Marlyn walking down the street all by herself." María was breathless with the news.

"Yes, María. You've seen a little girl in a pink dress walking down the street by herself?"

"Yes, a pink dress!"

"You have? When? Where?" exclaimed Grandma Edith in frantic joy.

"It was about an hour ago, a mile or so down the street. She said she was going home, to the next village."

Buoyed by the good news, the searchers flew down the street until they reached the section of the road María had told them about. There they began a careful door-to-door search, and the people at most of the houses excitedly joined the search. The only exception was the couple at one house: a sweet-faced woman and a man with a pencil mustache. Not only were they not helpful; they were downright nasty.

Grandma Edith searched and prayed, prayed and searched. The last thing she wanted to do was to have to go home and tell her daughter that her little girl was lost. Sick with remorse and fear, she finally was constrained to corral Frank and Wanda and get on the bus to go home—but not before notifying the police and the newspaper. She rummaged through her purse and dug out a picture of me to leave with each place.

Little Girl Lost

But before she left the police station, the police had a terrifying piece of news for her. "Señora Vega, I must tell you that there is a child kidnapping ring at work here in Guadalajara. Dozens of children have been abducted and sold to the underground market." This latest bit of news made an intolerable situation even more terrifying.

And then she had to head to the bus stop with Wanda and Frank and, once home, confess to her daughter the dreadful news that her baby girl had disappeared and could not be found. My mother listened in disbelief for several seconds before sinking onto a chair. "You looked everywhere? Where? Where is everywhere? Are you sure she wasn't just hiding under a bed or in a closet? You know what she's like! She could be anywhere!" Then, as the truth of the words she had just spoken hit her, she began sobbing. Yes, her little girl was adventurous, trusting, and utterly fearless, and therefore could be anywhere—*anywhere!*

"We looked in all those places several times, as well as at every house for miles around! But let's call Monrad! Surely he'll know what to do!" My father was president of the Guadalajara Mission. He had left that morning on a trip visiting churches and church members throughout the area and was not expected back for several weeks.

"Yes, yes, the conference officials will know where to find him; they have his itinerary. I'll call the mission office right away!"

The people at the conference were aghast at the news of the missing little girl and immediately began making telephone calls to locate my father. However, he was deep in the mountains on horseback, and all efforts to find him proved futile.

That news was the one-two punch for my mother that nearly finished her. Her baby girl was gone and no one could find her, and what was even worse, her husband was nowhere to be found. She was on her own, except for God.

Except for God! That was it! It was Wednesday; prayer meeting night, and most of the church members would be there. Together, they would form an invincible army. "Come, everyone, we're going to prayer meeting; it's almost time! Doña Triné, can you fix a quick bite to eat for the children? I'm not hungry. Are you, Grandma Edith? No, I didn't think so—but Frank and Wanda might be—get them fed, and after that they should probably change into clothes that aren't so dusty."

Prayer meeting that night was an agonizing supplication for the return

Beyond Ashes

of a little girl in a pink dress who was wound around the hearts of all the church members. Afterward Nacho Ponce, the mission treasurer, announced that he was going back to where I was last seen and would search until he found me. Nine-year-old Frank asked if he could go too. My mother and Señor Ponce both agreed, and the two drove off into the night in the treasurer's car.

No one slept that night. Grandma Edith stayed up all night storming heaven's gate for the safe return of her little Marlyn. Mamá was beside herself with misery and fear, so distraught that she became physically ill. Grandma Edith interrupted her prayer long enough to make an herbal drink for her, trying to calm her. It seemed to help, but not much. Even Wanda, only five years old, shared in the general distress. She kept sobbing, "The pool. She was playing in the pool. She must have gone in the pool and drowned. My fault. It's my fault because I wasn't watching her. Oh Jesus, please forgive me!"

Morning finally came. Red-eyed and exhausted, the family dressed for the day. Frank came in, dejected and spent: no Marlyn. Wanda went out and retrieved the daily newspaper from the front yard. "Look, Mamá, Marlyn is in the newspaper!" Mamá looked at the paper. Sure enough, there on the front page was the picture that Grandma had given the newspaper, along with a large banner headline: "*Niña Robada*" ("Kidnapped Girl") in large print. The story beneath the headline told of my disappearance and included the information, "The girl is an American citizen. The Mexican police will turn the kidnappers over to the American authorities, and the penalty for kidnapping in the United States is the death sentence." Mamá read the story rapidly, then handed it wordlessly to Grandma Edith. Grandma read it too, then said, "If someone has taken Marlyn, maybe ... maybe this will convince them to return her."

Suddenly loud pounding came from the front door. Rafa, one of the mission secretaries, had a story to tell. She had intended to pray all night, she told the two women, but fell asleep and had a dream. "I was in a field with sagebrush all around—and lots of holes in the ground. At the bottom of one of the holes there was Marlyn! Then I woke up suddenly. You know, I believe the Lord sent me this dream. When I told my sister, she laughed and said the dream was caused by indigestion. But I am sure she is wrong!"

Little Girl Lost

Grandma Edith and Mamá had been listening intently. Now they stood in thoughtful silence. Then Grandma Edith said, "It is from God."

"Yes," agreed Mamá. "He woke you up right away after the dream, so you would not forget it. This is how God does things."

Grandma Edith grabbed her purse and smoothed her hair with her hand. "I'm going, and I will look in every hole in that village until I find her! Rafa, will you join me? But Anita, I think you should stay here in case Monrad calls and you can tell him about the dream. You are the best one to be with Wanda and Frank to keep their spirits up." Rafa and Mamá both nodded their agreement.

Still sobbing, Mamá hugged Grandma Edith hard. "Go get Marlyn and bring her home!"

The bus ride to the village where I had been last seen seemed interminable. But before long they were there. News of the search quickly spread through the village, and the friendly villagers joined the search. Best of all, María showed up and volunteered to help. "Señoras," she told them, "there is a large company here that makes bricks. They dig holes in the ground to get the clay for them. There are many fields full of holes the brickmakers have left. I know where all the fields are, and we will look together until we find your little girl!"

With María's help, they worked their way through field after field, running from hole to hole in the hot sun, carrying walking sticks and working their way around the sagebrush. María was swift and it was hard to keep up with her, but urgency sped them on. The unpleasant-looking man with the pencil mustache appeared too, and said he might know what had happened to the little girl. "Some travelers on burros went past this morning, and they had a little girl with them that was crying loudly. I think it might have been your little girl." He gestured back the way Grandma and Rafa had come.

They thanked the man but kept on searching the holes. If the dream was from God as they believed, then they were going about their hunt the right way. And that man did not seem trustworthy!

So many fields, so many holes, but no little girl! It was afternoon when, on the way to yet another field, they encountered an elderly man. "We are looking for a three-year-old girl wearing a pink dress. We think she might be in a hole in one of the fields around here. Do you have any idea where she might be?"

Beyond Ashes

"Sí, Señora." The old man stroked his chin thoughtfully. "Early this morning I saw a woman dump a burlap sack into a hole. Who knows? Your little girl could be in that sack! Follow me! I can take you to the place!" He took off at a trot through a path overgrown with manzanita, and the three women struggled to keep up with him, bending low to get through the manzanita. They were worn out by the all-day search and caked in sweat and dust. Eventually, the manzanita ended and they found themselves in a field of sagebrush and holes. It was exactly the way Rafa had seen it in her dream!

The old man pointed. "Try that hole over there." And then—he simply vanished. Rafa ran over to the hole he had indicated and let out a scream. "Over here! There's something at the bottom of this hole!" Grandma and María rushed over and looked down at the little girl in a pink dress, burlap tangled around her legs and feet. María, the youngest and nimblest, lowered herself into the hole and handed up the child. "¡La niñita perdida fue encontrada!" ("The little lost girl has been found!") The message spread through the watching crowd.

"Is she OK?" That was the next question. Yes, still breathing! But the child was unconscious and the little body was hot, far too hot. Grandma Edith carried me as the three women ran to the police station to share the good news and ask for help getting me to the mission hospital. The police found some cool cloths to place on my head, and then Grandma Edith, Rafa, and I were treated to a high-speed ride to the mission hospital at Guadalajara, sirens blaring. I didn't get to enjoy it, however, because I was still unconscious; I had been drugged.

At the hospital the nurses placed me in an ice-filled bath to bring down my temperature. The doctor shook his head, incredulous. "Her temperature is 105, and she has heatstroke. Another hour in that hole and we'd have lost her. All I can say is that you are very lucky to have this child alive!"

María, the dream, the old man—the timing was all perfect. God's hand was in all of it. I was lost, but never truly lost, for God knew where I was all along, and He showed my whereabouts to those who loved me.

Time and time again, I have lost my way and blundered into circumstances that could have proved my ruin. But I have never been lost to God; always He has known where I was. Time after time He has pulled me back to Him, and He has rescued me for a life of service to His cause.

Little Girl Lost

He also brought me up out of a horrible pit,
Out of the miry clay,
And set my feet upon a rock,
And established my steps (Psalm 40:2, NKJV).

CHAPTER 2

California, Here We Come!

Mamá would scarcely let me out of her sight in the months following the kidnapping. I can't say that I blamed her. I would have been the same way. And it seemed the experience, including whatever they had drugged me with, had knocked the spunk out of me. I would lie listlessly on the floor or the sofa. After work at the mission office each day, Mamá would massage my arms and legs and cook food especially for me.

The police eventually told us that the sweet-faced woman and the unpleasant man owned the brickmaking operation in Zapopan and, most importantly, were in charge of the child-trafficking ring in that region. Apparently, the newspaper article frightened them into dumping me in that hole and leaving me to die there. They suddenly vanished, and the authorities never were able to find them.

As I was recovering from my lethargic state, Papá was fighting a battle of his own. Somewhere in his travels he had acquired amoebic dysentery, and now he could not shake it off. He had been sick plenty of times before: he'd had malaria, blackwater fever, and once while sleeping on the ground, he was stung by a bark scorpion and saved by Indians, who buried him in the ground so the mud could pull out the lethal venom. And with the help of God he had always pulled through.

This time, though, was different. Dysentery is never fun, but these days it does not usually kill people. However, the amoeba had gotten into Papá's bloodstream and affected his internal organs, and now he clearly wasn't able to carry the workload he had always managed in the past. It was hard for Mamá to watch her husband struggle each day to do his job. Unable to digest his food properly, he had grown gaunt and pale—skeletal compared to the man he had been. The process had been going on for several years, but he was never a man to complain or take it easy when there was work to be done. Now, though, it was obvious to everyone, even him, that if he was to survive, he must rest and get proper medical attention. He finally put in a request to the General Conference for a leave of absence. His doctor seconded the request, writing, "It will take quite a long pull to rebuild his vitality and nutrition. He will be able to do light work, but there will be at least one year of careful management necessary to bring about the desired result."

Then one day Papá got the letter he was waiting for. His request had been approved! There was sudden excitement in the house—we were moving to the United States!

"What is the United States?" I wanted to know.

"It's where we're going," I was told. "Papá will get well there, and you will make new friends!"

Doña Triné sat down on the floor with Wanda and me and helped us go through our dolls and toys, deciding which ones we loved enough to take with us to the United States and which ones we would give away. We packed up the toys and the clothes we had outgrown and took them to the Dorcas Society to give away to poor people.

Some men came to our house and started packing things. We couldn't take very much, because we would be living in a tiny trailer. We were leaving most of our furniture to the family that would be taking over Papá's job. But I was too excited to mourn the loss of our possessions very much.

The day finally came when the seven of us went down to the train station: Mamá, Papá, Grandma Edith, Great-grandma María, and we three children—Frank, Wanda, and I. Doña Triné and our housekeeper, Doña Goyita, hugged and hugged us, wiping tears from their eyes. I was sad to be leaving them, but I was also jumping up and down with excitement. I had never been on a train before! We climbed the tall steps onto the train, and Papá found us a place to sit. I immediately claimed a window seat. The car we were in trembled a little bit, and I shivered deliciously. The whistle blew and slowly the train started, then picked up speed as we pulled out of the station. And then we were out in the open country. I stared at the rolling hills, the small villages, and the Sierra Madre mountains, range on range, the farthest dissolving into blue mist.

At train stops, native Indians would stand dressed in colorful clothes with large baskets perched on their heads, coaxing us to buy food or

California, Here We Come!

homemade wares. Grandma Edith was skilled at bartering and purchased some chattering parrots and Mexican dolls for Frank and Wanda and me. Of course, Papá said we could keep them; we'd find a space somewhere in our cramped new living quarters.

That night Wanda and I slept with our heads on Mamá's lap. Late the next day, somewhat rumpled and tired, we arrived in Nogales, Arizona, where Papá had church business to take care of. Frank begged to be allowed to stay with Papá and was given permission, on condition that he help with carrying things.

National City adventures
The next morning the five of us boarded the train again for the final eight-hour ride to National City. As the train pulled into the station, everyone began gathering up their belongings, with Mamá handing some to Wanda and even me to carry.

We climbed off the train into a sea of people, and there to greet us were Mr. and Mrs. Moon. Their hair was silvery, their faces kind. I liked them right away. They had served in Mexico as missionaries for many years, so they understood us better than most Americans would have. It was especially nice that they spoke Spanish. They took us to their home and helped us get settled in the tiny trailer on their property.

That first morning in America, I woke up, stretched, and looked out the window of our little trailer. Flower petals drifted across a sunny swath of lawn, and palm trees swayed at its edge. Chickadees and nuthatches flitted about, chirping cheerfully. I jumped up and ran outside. I liked our new home!

Mrs. Moon, who soon became "Grandma" to us children, came walking across the yard. "Come on over and have some breakfast!" she called out. Realizing that we had not had time to go out and buy food, she had prepared a wonderful meal for us: fruit, cereal, toast, and scrambled eggs. Mr. Moon, our new "Grandpa," told us about National City while we ate. "I'll take you to see the church and hospital a little later. And speaking of the hospital, have you thought about work? With your training, Anita, employment at the hospital might be something to explore. That or the nursing home; you actually might like the nursing home better, because it's right next door and you could keep an eye on the children."

"Of course, I can watch them while you work, Anita," Mrs. Moon interjected. "You don't need to worry on that account. But I know how it is—you like to be as close to your children as possible when you work."

"And a big plus for you is that they are always looking for good workers who are fluent in Spanish," Mr. Moon added. Mamá looked up from her plate and smiled. I saw that she liked the idea.

It didn't take long to put away the few belongings we had brought with us. Mamá went out to buy some supplies, and Wanda and I went out to explore our new home. It was delightful! A fat squirrel ran partway up a tree, stopped, jerked his tail a few times, and then resumed his climb. Butterflies skimmed and dipped amid the irises and tiger lilies. A soft salt breeze blew in from the ocean.

We eventually went back to the trailer. Mamá was back; she had hung the birdcages holding the two parrots Grandma Edith had bought onto hooks on the side of the trailer and was now hanging up clothes in the pint-sized closet. Grandma Edith was sitting at the tiny table, making sandwiches for lunch. I asked for a drink, and Mamá went to the sink to get me one. But in order for us to get to the sink, Grandma Edith and Wanda had to step aside for us to get through.

We ate lunch, crowded around the tiny table, with me on Mamá's lap. After lunch the three women got up to clear the table but quickly discovered that in this trailer, kitchen duty was a job for just one person—more would not fit in the spot by the sink. So Wanda and I went back to our sleeping area and sat on the bed to be out of everyone's way. The two grandmas went outside and strolled around the enormous lawn, leaving Mamá to clear away our lunch. Living in a space this small was going to take a lot of cooperation!

We eventually got to the place where if one person needed to walk through the trailer from one end to the other, the rest of us automatically moved to one side and compressed ourselves to let the person through.

A few days later, Papá and Frank were back. Papá, looking more haggard than ever, sank into a chair, exhausted. Frank, though, was excited about his adventure with Papá.

"I woke up and Papá was stabbing at it with his knife. I was afraid it would get away, but it didn't. Papá wouldn't let it!"

"What was it?" we girls asked together, as if we had rehearsed it.

"It was this long," he continued, holding up his hands two feet apart. "And it had pretty red and yellow and black stripes around it!"

California, Here We Come!

"WHAT WAS IT?" the three women demanded.

"What? Oh, it was a snake."

"Oh my goodness!" Mamá exclaimed. "Was it poisonous?"

"It was a coral snake," Papá said quietly. "One bite and you are history." He was far too weary to jump up and down and yell like Frank was doing. "So before climbing onto my own cot I thought I'd better check it out too. And there under the pillow was an even bigger coral snake. I tell you, it was a real fight to slice his head off with my knife, but in the end I got him."

"No wonder you look tired," Mamá exclaimed, stroking his head.

"I didn't sleep at all that night. I didn't even dare turn off the light. I just sat there with my knife, watching for any more of those things. I had no idea how they were getting into the room. All I could do was watch."

"Come on, Monnie, let's go to bed. You need a long, long rest. There are no coral snakes here, I guarantee!" Mamá told him.

So life in California began. Mamá started work at the nursing home, where her competence and caring spirit won her a multitude of friends. As we made our own friends and learned English from them, Mamá became Mama and Papá became Daddy, and our daddy was bit by bit regaining his health at the nearby Paradise Valley Sanitarium. Frank was enrolled in the neighboring church school, riding his bike the mile there and back each day.

I remember those as the delicious days: days spent out in the sweet warm air, running through the grass, watching the birds and squirrels, and clambering around on the strong arms of our favorite climbing tree—a great pepper tree at the edge of the property. Around the perimeter of the property stood apricot trees, quince trees, and sweet wild grapes. We would pick bucketsful and take them to Mama. From the quinces, Mama would make *atole*, a Spanish drink that is thick and sweet like a smoothie.

The day came when, after a month in the sanitarium, our daddy returned home. We children clustered around him, hugging him all at once. How good it was to see him no longer looking so pallid and gaunt! He still had to receive outpatient care, but now he could be a stay-at-home dad. He warmed to the task, buying seeds and working with us to plant lettuce, tomatoes, potatoes, beans, and more. Our garden flourished year-round, and we practically lived off it. He economized in other ways too. He would buy five pounds of honey from a local beekeeper, and from a nearby discount store a huge jar of peanut butter and large bunches of bananas. Peanut butter-honey-banana sandwiches became a staple of our diet.

Still, it was a hard time for our family, and every little bit helped. Once Mama got home from work at three each afternoon, Daddy put on his suit most days and went to work as a literature evangelist, selling Christian books door-to-door. And sometimes he would preach in nearby Escondido. Mama would pack a picnic lunch of chili beans, sandwiches, and potato salad. After the church service we'd find a spot where we could spread a tablecloth under a large, spreading tree and eat a picnic lunch.

Daddy believed in the importance of work. In Mexico, with him gone so much of the time and Mama working at the mission office, most of the housekeeping and childcare had been done by servants. As a result, we children had had almost no responsibilities. Daddy's system was a lot different. We had our assignments according to age and ability, and we each received a small allowance. I would save my pennies to buy a candy bar—back then they cost only a nickel.

Grandma Edith moved to Tijuana, where she used her energies in building up the local church and also teaching children in the neighborhood and doctoring the sick, using herbs and natural methods. We children were sad to see the parrots go with her, but we got to see them when we visited her, taking turns one week at a time—and oh how we loved those visits! Grandma Edith would have us join her class of schoolchildren and teach us Spanish. She wanted to make sure we didn't forget how to speak Spanish.

Then Great-grandma María traveled to Tijuana to be with Grandma Edith so she could help with her work. While Grandma Edith was off working during the day, Great-grandma María would care for the fastidiously groomed yard, clean the house, and prepare the meals. Great-grandma María was special to me, and I always believed that I was special to her as well. She stood tall, slender, and ramrod-straight. She loved being outside, and as she knelt on the grass, working the ground in their garden with a trowel, I would sit beside her, digging in the dirt with my own small trowel. Walking through the neighborhood together, we would hold hands while she softly hummed. We'd pick mangoes and papayas and eat them, and then we'd have beauty shop sessions, with me brushing her long hair and braiding it for her, and her brushing out my hair and setting it on rag rollers.

California, Here We Come!

Mama was moving more slowly these days, and we children knew why: Mama was going to have another baby! One night Mama tiptoed into our room and whispered that she and Daddy were leaving for the hospital and Frank was in charge. By the time we woke up the next morning, Daddy was back with the thrilling announcement that we had a new baby sister—Mildred!

From the start she was Millie to us. Her hair was dark, her cheeks chubby, her skin a flawless olive color. I was only four years old, too little to take care of Millie, but Wanda was six. She loved helping out with Millie's care. From the beginning the two of them shared a special bond.

Little by little Daddy was getting well. No longer shuffling, he now walked briskly about his work, and his face began to be ruddy with health. He was doing so well, in fact, that he was asked to pastor a church in Tijuana and start a Spanish-speaking church in a neighboring town. But that would mean being away from home a lot, the way things used to be. Now that he was getting a taste of what it was like to be with his family, he didn't want to let go of the experience. He wound up taking a job as a nurse at Paradise Valley Sanitarium.

Just six weeks after Millie was born, Mama had to return to work. Mama and Daddy arranged it so that she worked days from seven to three and Daddy worked afternoons and evenings from three to eleven. That way one of them could almost always be home with us, and if for some reason they couldn't be, the Moons were happy to watch us.

If we loved the arrangement, Daddy loved it even more. I remember his soft, happy laughter as he bathed Millie in the sink, then dressed her and walked outside with Millie and me—Wanda was in school now. Millie would squeal in glee as he tossed her in the air. Then he'd do the same with me, even though I was a big four-year-old. It was a side of him I hadn't seen much of before, what with his being gone so much and then being so sick in Mexico.

It was becoming increasingly evident that I was accident-prone. For instance, one day Wanda, Frank, and I were outside playing hide-and-seek when I tripped over a live wire and fell down, unconscious. Frank grabbed my leg but quickly dropped it as the electricity surged through his body. He and Wanda stood there screaming, "Marlyn! Marlyn! Wake up!" Mama heard their screams and came running. Seeing what was going on, she grabbed a stick and used it to roll me off the wire.

"Mama, is Marlyn dead? What happened to her?" Mama grabbed my arm and searched for a pulse. There was one, but it was faint and irregular.

"She isn't dead, but I'm afraid she soon will be if God doesn't work a miracle. Let's all pray as hard as we can!" The nearby sanitarium didn't have an emergency room, so it was God or nothing. After several minutes of earnest joint intercession, Mama saw a fluttering eyelid, then a jerking leg. She scooped me up and carried me into the trailer, and by suppertime, I was almost back to normal.

A new house
It was becoming more and more evident that we had to have a bigger place to live. A living arrangement that had almost worked with three children was unmanageable with four. In a tiny trailer, the place got dirty so fast! In no time at all, it would be cluttered and the floor too dirty for little Millie, who was crawling everywhere. Of course, it only took a few minutes to tidy, sweep, and run a mop over the floor, but then a couple of hours later it had to be done all over again! And with things so crowded, especially when it rained, sooner or later someone would step on Millie's hand or trip over her, and she would howl.

We all started praying for a bigger house, and Daddy started watching for suitable property he could buy—suitable meaning close to work and school and inexpensive. Our prayers were answered when a lot became available just a mile from the school Frank and Wanda (and eventually I) attended, as well as from the nursing home and sanitarium where Mama and Daddy worked. The best part? Daddy was able to negotiate the deal for a price of $700. Even back then, that was a great buy!

Now all we needed was a house to go on the property. Later that year Daddy came across a newspaper ad for army base houses for sale. These were pretty basic, but with a skilled carpenter and a talented interior decorator in the family, that wouldn't necessarily be a problem. So Daddy selected a house and bought it.

I remember standing with Wanda and Frank on a knoll a safe distance from the lot, watching rocks and dirt flying everywhere as dynamite blasted a large rectangular hole for the basement. Once the basement was complete, the house itself was relocated to our lot and gently lowered into place atop the basement. Then an outdoor toilet was temporarily installed and a large tent was erected, and we all moved into the tent to be near the house.

California, Here We Come!

Mama and Daddy worked on the house several hours every day. Daddy constructed two bedrooms in our new basement: a big one for us three girls, and a smaller one for Frank. Upstairs he knocked out walls and built new ones to create a new kitchen, a living room, a bedroom for him and Mama, and a bathroom we all used. Mama painted, with some help from Frank, and picked out flooring, which Daddy installed. Then Mama made curtains and picked out beautiful—to my eyes, at least—secondhand furniture. Before the winter rains began, our new house was ready to become a home. One happy day we abandoned the tent and moved in. After living all cramped up together for nearly a year and a half, our new home seemed unbelievably spacious.

Time passed, and it was time for me to enter first grade. Oh, how I loved school! Mrs. Fuller was my first-grade teacher at San Diego Union Academy, a church school in National City. I loved the stories, the coloring, and cutting out and pasting; but best of all I was actually learning to read! We lived just a mile from the school, and Frank, who was in sixth grade now, would give Wanda and me a ride to and from school on his bicycle. He would take each of us one block at a time, dropping the first one off, then going back and getting the other one, until he got us safely to school or home.

One day after school while I was still in first grade, I went running across the street about five feet behind Wanda. Mama was on the other side of the street, walking toward us to meet us and take us home. Following Wanda, I ran behind a school bus that was parked beside the street. A car was coming from the other direction and the driver could not see me nor I her, because of the bus. I ran smack into the side of the passing car and wound up flat on my back on the pavement. I opened my eyes in time to see the horrified face of the woman driving the car and heard Mama's frantic scream. Mama told me afterward that when she saw me running into the street, she prayed, screamed, and covered her eyes all at the same time. Then when she opened her eyes, she saw me lying on the pavement and thought for sure I had been hit. Once more we saw that God had been looking after me.

"Pour out your heart like water before the face of the Lord. Lift your hands toward Him for the life of your young children" (Lamentations 2:19, NKJV).

CHAPTER 3

Seven Is the Perfect Number

Something new was in the offing: the most wonderful gift I had ever been given. Its first indication came on a warm summer morning in July before the break of dawn, though I didn't yet know what it presaged. Mama poked Daddy. "Monnie, wake up. I'm hungry for tacos. Please get up and get me some tacos."

Startled, Daddy sat up. "What? Anita, are you pregnant?" He knew what it meant when Mama craved something.

"I don't know ... Monnie ... Tacos, ¡rápido por favor!" (Mama was trying to learn English, and she often mixed Spanish with English when she talked.)

Yanking on his trousers, Daddy wondered where in the world he could find tacos this early in the morning. "OK, Anita. OK—I'll get some."

Opening the door, Daddy stretched out his arms into the early summer morning and inhaled the fresh air. He had to shade his eyes against the brilliant rising sun. Birds were everywhere, chirping below and soaring above his head. Trees swayed in the honeysuckle-laden breeze. It was going to be a fine day!

He chuckled as he climbed in the car, remembering the old wives' tale that when an expectant mother craved spicy food it meant the baby would be a boy. *Oh, yes, please God, let it be a baby and let it be a boy.* Good thing, he mused, that at six o'clock in the morning, there's not much traffic. Nothing could be found in National City. At last, he found an all-night Mexican restaurant in San Diego.

The doctor confirmed that Mama was pregnant, but our parents kept it a secret. Then one evening, Millie and I were playing on the floor in the living room with our dolls. Mama got down on the floor, picked up a doll, and began to sing "I have a little baby, I have a little baby. It's inside my tummy. It's inside my tummy," to the tune of the Spanish lullaby "A

La Ru-ru Niño." Daddy grinned from ear to ear.

"A baby in your tummy?" I asked.

"A baby, a baby!" Millie jumped up and down.

"A baby? When, Mama?" Wanda, who had been sitting on the sofa, dropped her knitting.

"The doctor said in March. My tummy is growing straight out like when I carried Frank. I think I'm going to have a boy."

"In March? On my birthday? A boy?" I danced with hopeful merriment.

"Que será, será," Mama laughed.

The day I turned seven, Mama's belly looked like a giant watermelon. She placed my hand on her belly, and I could feel the baby move.

"Your birthday present is still wrapped in my tummy, but the way he is kicking, I think he will be born soon."

Ten days later, on the sixteenth of March, Daddy rushed Mama to the hospital in the wee hours of the morning, and baby Milton was born. As was the custom in those days, Mama stayed in the hospital for several days. Waiting in the driveway for Daddy to bring Milton and Mama home, I looked around me. Nature was full of babies! Irises sent exploratory fingers up through the soil; birds worked at nest-building. My hands explored the overhanging branches of the apricot tree to find the swelling buds that would soon crack open to release flowers with soft petals.

Finally our car pulled into the driveway. A tingle ran throughout my body, sending a rush of excitement such as I had never felt before. When I saw the baby's plump little face, I couldn't think about or acknowledge anything else around me—the world seemed to stop and hold its place in time, just for that perfect moment.

"Hi, Milton, I'm your big sissy." My hands quivered as I slowly reached out to touch his little fingers. When his fingers grasped mine—a firm grip—I knew he was strong. I ran the tips of my fingers gently across his smooth face. I fell in love.

Our family of six was now a family of seven. We crowded around Mama. "Make room," Daddy chided, "we're coming through," as he guided Mama, holding the sweet bambino, to walk inside and sit down on the sofa.

I ran and sat beside her. "Mama, can he be my baby?"

"Well, as soon as I am strong enough I'll be going back to work.

Seven Is the Perfect Number

Wanda looks out for Millie kind of like she's her second mama, and since Millie's only three years old, Wanda's hands are plenty full. Yes, you are old enough now to help me with Milton. You can be his second mama."

"Oh Mama, can I hold him?" I squealed with excitement.

Mama gently placed Milton on my lap and showed me how to cradle his neck. "Be careful not to touch the soft spot on top of his head," she pointed. "You will have to wait until he is big and strong before you can play with him."

"Yes, Mama, I'll wait," I promised.

"He weighs nine pounds, just like you when you were born, and he kind of looks like you." She stroked my arm.

Milton radiated happiness from the start. Naturally inquisitive, he looked at every moment as a new adventure. I beamed with sisterly pride. He was my joy, my adorable baby brother, a replica of me. I beamed at the thought. Sometimes I would walk softly into the boys' room during the day and watch him as he napped, the tenderness within me so strong it hurt.

He grew so fast! One day I came home from school to see Milton on his tummy on the floor, slowly scooting along by pushing himself forward with his toes—a first attempt to crawl. As he grew and learned how to pull himself up on the crib, he would jump up and down with excitement, wanting to play. At feeding time, Milton was energetic. He would gulp the bite down and eagerly open his mouth for another bite just like a baby robin. He ate most everything, but when it came to green beans, he would grab the spoon, offer it to me, and then laugh. He was a sweet bundle of merriment—a mixture of joy and hilarity—a little brother who loved the out-of-doors just like me. Mama said I must watch Milton carefully. I must never let him out of my sight. He must never wander off and get lost the way I had.

I did watch him carefully. Sometimes he would hide. I would look for him and then he would jump out and say, "Boo!" Sometimes he got into my things. Oh how he could wreck my room. No matter, he was my little shadow. I didn't mind.

The convertible

School was out for the summer. Mama and Daddy had been saving their shekels and had bought a new car—a convertible. It was a used car, and Daddy got a good deal because the top had been damaged and there was a hole right above the front seat. Of course, in California it never rains in the summer, but once summer is over, it does rain—and how!

One evening at family worship, Daddy said, "We have to get a new top for the convertible before the rain comes, but there is no money. School is about to start, and there is enough money to pay tuition for Frank, Wanda, and Marlyn. But after we pay the tuition there will not be enough money to buy a new top for the convertible. We are just going to have to ask God to help us." And every night, that's what we did.

About a week later, some workmen in dusty clothes came knocking on our door. "Begging your pardon, sir," a short stocky man who looked to be the leader said, "we're going to be dynamiting in that field over there"—he gestured toward the big field next to our house—"and it would be safer if you all stay inside until we get done. But not to worry, we will keep a safe distance from your house. We will be very careful."

Knowing the danger, Daddy made sure we all stayed safely inside, though we did enjoy watching the earth and rocks flying every which way each time the workmen released a charge. Then all of a sudden—"Wow! Did you see that?" exclaimed Frank.

"What? What?" I had missed it.

"That was a big sucker! Landed smack-dab on top of our new car!" We three children went dashing out to the car to investigate. There, sitting primly on the driver's seat, was a big rock, and above it was the hole, no longer small. In fact, it was enormous!

Looking up, I saw the workmen sprinting across the field toward us. They surveyed the damage with chagrin. The man in charge said to Daddy, who had strolled out to investigate, "Sir, I can't tell you how sorry I am this happened. Of course our company will buy you a new top for your car."

Daddy, grinning, told him how Jesus had answered our prayers. The workman was flabbergasted. He exclaimed, "Why, in all of my years of working with dynamite, I have never seen a rock fly so far—an angel must have carried it in answer to your prayers. I am happy to have had a part in that answer!"

A dozen stitches

Frank and Millie shared an affinity for animals. Frank found a stray black Labrador dog, and it became our family pet. We named him Big Boy.

Seven Is the Perfect Number

Frank built a cage and raised doves, and Millie helped with their care. They also enjoyed finding injured squirrels, rabbits, and birds and nursing them back to health. I delighted being with Millie now that she was four years old. We would sit under the trees for hours playing with dolls.

Mama and Daddy had taught Wanda to cook, and she was quite good at it, so she was put in charge of cooking one meal a day. I had learned to do basic housework, so I assumed the role of assistant housekeeper. Frank was put in charge of keeping us girls entertained. He was very good at this, and we loved the ideas he came up with. He would collapse old cardboard packing boxes, which we used as sleds to slide down a large hill next to our house. He'd give us rides on his bike and play tag with us. He also brought his friends over after school to play baseball in our field. He could pack a wallop to the ball. I loved to watch them play, and I loved having him as my big brother.

One day as I watched them play, I occupied myself with my own little ball. At one point the ball escaped and went rolling toward home plate. Frank was up to bat, and, not wanting my ball to get in his way, I went running after it. Suddenly there was a bolt of pain and everything went black.

I came to at the hospital, head exploding with pain like none I'd ever felt before. Daddy sat next to me, looking all wobbly like things seen from afar on a very hot day. His face was ashen. A man was talking to him but his voice was all wrong; it sounded the way voices did on a phonograph that was giving out—distorted and slow. I thought I heard him say, "She can sleep but wake her up every two or three hours to check." I slid back into unconsciousness as someone put me in a wheelchair.

At home again, I mostly slept, waking up briefly from time to time. Always there were anxious faces around me. Frank crying, saying how sorry he was. Daddy saying he knew it wasn't Frank's fault. Daddy telling Mama how miraculous it was that Frank's bat had hit my head just a hairline away from my left temple.

Finally I woke up to find things looking and sounding normal again. "What happened, Daddy?" I asked.

"Thank God you're back! You got hit in the head with a bat, Frank's bat. He's been feeling awful, thinking he killed you, but it wasn't his fault; he just didn't see you there. I went running to you when I heard all the boys screaming."

Beyond Ashes

"Oh Daddy, I was just trying to get my ball out of his way—"

"It was just one of those things that happen, sweetheart. You sure had me scared, though! Blood was spurting everywhere, and Frank was putting pressure on the wound all the way to the hospital, trying to keep you from losing all your blood. And me, I was praying all the way there. And did you know your head is all sewed up like a baseball? You have a dozen stitches in your head! Thank God you're OK!"

So that's what happened! No wonder they called me a cat with nine lives. I lay there thinking about it and wondering how many of my nine lives I had used up!

Time was passing. I was now nine years old, Milton was two, Millie was now five, Wanda was eleven, and Frank had just turned fifteen. That summer, life was about to change again—and how!

"The Lord will watch over your coming and going both now and forevermore" (Psalm 121:8, NIV).

CHAPTER 4

New Places, New Faces

Mama and Daddy were becoming concerned about harmful influences from families that had moved to the area. My parents always put their children first, so they began praying for guidance as to what to do.

One of Daddy's coworkers told him about a lovely little town called Weimar, tucked away in the foothills of the California Sierras. It was full of beauty, both historic and natural, and was a wonderful place to raise children, she said, adding that building sites were available at very reasonable prices; in fact, her own family had bought a parcel of land and was planning to move there.

Mama and Daddy made it a matter of much prayer as they investigated the situation. Daddy visited the area and talked with the real estate agents handling property sales in the area. He returned home with the mind-boggling announcement that he had bought a one-hundred-year-old two-story farmhouse set on ten acres of wooded land—gotten it at a scandalously low price—and we would be moving soon!

What? Moving away from all my friends? But I was always up for adventure; in fact, our entire family was that way. Daddy put our house on the market, and in no time at all it sold. We hired a moving van and began packing.

Northern California, we children quickly discovered, was not at all like Southern California. First, were the trees. Proper trees had a long bald trunk with fronded leaves sprouting out of the top in lovely dishevelment. *These* trees had millions of peculiar-looking leaves, long and narrow like hypodermic needles. In fact, they were *called* needles! The trees were wide at the bottom and narrow on top, sort of triangular. I loved their sharp, pungent smell.

There were oak trees, too, and a barn, a fence to corral some goats we acquired, a chicken coop—we bought some chickens too—and a well. Best of all, from us kids' point of view, was the large concrete water tank, eight feet deep and ten feet in diameter, where we were allowed to swim.

I still remembered the Sierra Madre from Mexico. Now we lived next door to their northern counterpart: the Sierra Nevada. Sometimes after church we would drive up into those mountains. I had never experienced anything like the aromatic smell of those pine forests.

We quickly settled into the old farmhouse. This was as spacious and rambling as the trailer where we had once lived was tiny. The boys had a large upstairs bedroom to themselves, and the girls likewise. It had an old-fashioned charm to it, like a distinguished old lady in a ruffled gown. It did need paint and wallpaper, but after the work we had done to the army base house, we were skilled in those areas.

Of course we had a garden—a huge one! We all worked together on it during the summer. Unlike National City, Northern California could grow only one crop a year, but we still managed to eat from it all year round, as Wanda and I helped can its bounty. We children were responsible for feeding all the livestock as well as for milking the goats and collecting the chicken eggs. We helped with the housework, too, and when Daddy needed help outside, he would often call on me and on Milton too, once he was a little older.

Our two dogs, Kaiser and Jip, loved our new home. Jip was a small black mongrel, and Kaiser was half German shepherd and half chow; he was built like a German shepherd and colored like a chow. He loved to roam the hills and once came home with a face-full of porcupine quills. Another time he came home smelling like a skunk!

Mama and Daddy both found work at the Weimar Sanitarium. The Weimar church school, though small, was a good school, and Daddy got me enrolled in fourth grade and Wanda in sixth. I liked my teacher, Mr. Heath.

We joined a church in Meadow Vista—a friendly church with about one hundred members and a couple dozen teenagers. It was a lively, active church with plenty of activities for us kids: parties, Pathfinders, youth meetings, caroling through the neighborhood at Christmas, and ushering and giving special music at church. In no time at all I had plenty of friends.

New Places, New Faces

From charades to chatter

At eighteen months old, Milton had not been attempting too much speech. His name for our pet dog was *Atoo* and for our calico cat, *Atootoo*. Although he wasn't attempting to talk, his problem-solving skills seemed noticeably more advanced than those of most other children his age. He was obviously very bright and understood everything anyone said.

Milton communicated to us with his own version of sign language. More and more it became a way of entertaining his older siblings, like playing a game of charades. His eyes would sparkle when we guessed right. However, Mama and Daddy were not amused and were considering taking him to a speech therapist.

One day when our parents had driven into town, I said, "Milton, you are three years old. Mama and Daddy are thinking about taking you to a speech therapist. But I know that you *can* talk, and it's time for you to start. When Mama and Daddy return from town, here is what you can say: 'Mama and Daddy, I'm so happy you are home.'" We practiced the sentence a few times.

At the sound of the car in the driveway, Milton ran outside and danced around the car. "Mama and Daddy, I'm so happy you are home! Mama and Daddy, I'm so happy you are home!"

Mama and Daddy wrapped him up in their arms and hugged him tight. After that Milton chattered constantly with an amazing vocabulary for a three-year-old.

Although Milton was cheerfully optimistic and maintained a generous attitude in our family circle, sometimes when I would have to get after him, he would say, "OK, Mama," and then teasingly mimic what I said. He copied everything I did. I didn't want to let him down, so I carefully watched my every move. If I ignored my chores, he ignored his. If I cut corners, he followed suit. I tried to be a good example.

Hard work pays off

"Daddy, I'm so hot and itchy! Can I go for a swim in the river?"

"Of course, Marlyn. We'll all go after supper, provided we meet our daily goal by then. For now, get yourself a drink of water and keep on hoeing."

It was hot, exhausting work, but I did enjoy working alongside my parents and siblings. Daddy had contracted with the State of California to work in a state program for management of white pine blister rust in the Sierra Nevada mountain range above Emigrant Gap. Blister rust is a fungus disease that attacks pine trees, but it requires a host plant, which in that part of the country was gooseberry. Get rid of the gooseberry, and soon you are rid of the rust.

We were assigned a territory to clear of gooseberry bushes. Each of us had a two-pronged hoe. Five days a week, we worked hard, ripping the gooseberry plants from the earth and forming great piles of them. Daddy and Frank tackled the largest bushes, which sometimes grew as big as trees. Housewives made pies out of them; we, however, got to the point where we never wanted to see another one!

When we were done for the day, we'd trek down the mountainside to our camp, where Mama had a feast for us, cooked over our campfire: chili beans, baked potatoes, and cornbread were some of our favorites. And then we'd go swimming in the river that we were camped beside, swimming, splashing, and laughing. By summer's end we had cleared our assigned area.

Daddy tithed our family's earnings and then distributed the rest to the various family members. He paid me fifty dollars for my part in the work, the most money I had ever earned in my life! We children were tasked with buying our school clothes with our earnings. I decided to buy mine at Goodwill. I shopped carefully, and in the end was able to get more clothes for half the price I would have paid at a department store.

At the end of my fourth-grade year, the little church school I had been attending closed because of low enrollment. There was a good church school in Auburn, ten miles beyond Meadow Vista, but no bus ran there, and with Mama and Daddy both working, there was no way for us to get to that school. So Wanda and I began attending public school, riding the school bus to Meadow Vista.

Experiences with local wildlife

"Middle children make their own way": it's a saying that applies to me. I loved taking long solitary walks, humming to myself. Mama and Daddy had no objections as long as I took Kaiser with me and walked on the path along the irrigation canal so I could not get lost. One day, on a walk, I was startled to see a large antlered deer charging at me full tilt! Did he think I wanted to abscond with his wife and children? There wasn't time

New Places, New Faces

to ponder the question. I turned and sprinted away, faster than I had ever run before. The sound of thudding hooves eventually died away, and I was safe.

Nancy, who lived nearby, was becoming my best summertime friend. An only child, she loved spending time at our house, where so much was always going on. She'd help me do my chores so we could run out to play. Down on the other end of our property was an irrigation ditch, our favorite place to play. We gathered big rocks and made a dam to create a pool, where we had fun wading and splashing in the water.

One spring day when we arrived, the pool was jumping with tadpoles. They had such cute tails!

"How long before they're frogs?" I asked.

"Not long. It just takes a couple weeks."

Day after day we hiked down to the irrigation ditch to admire the tadpoles. I had no idea they grew so fast. "I wish we could have them where we could watch them grow better," I said. "Because wouldn't it be great if we got to watch them when they turn into little frogs?"

The two of us raced back to the house, where we found several large jars, and we filled them with tadpoles. Then we glided smoothly up to the water tank, taking care not to spill any of our tadpole water, and climbed up to the top. *Splash!* Fifty-seven tadpoles now occupied the water tank. But the tank was far from full, so we knew we would need lots more tadpoles to fill it properly. We made six or seven more trips, and in the end we were quite impressed with our tadpole aquarium.

It was fun to watch our tadpoles begin their ascent into frogs. Gradually their little bodies began to take shape, their legs began to grow, and their tails shortened each day. One day when we climbed up the ladder and looked into the water, the metamorphosis was complete: the tank was hopping with tiny frogs!

But wait: where hundreds of tadpoles had swarmed, now there were mere dozens. "What happened? Where'd they go?" Nancy demanded. She got the answer a minute later, when three little frogs leaped out of the tank and plopped onto the ground eight feet below. Were they killed by the fall? Nope! They had landed on all fours and immediately started jumping toward—oh no! The kitchen!

Nancy and I climbed down the ladder as fast as we could and raced into the kitchen. The place was hopping with frogs! I screamed as my

Beyond Ashes

foot landed on something squishy, making me slip and fall down smack on my back. I carefully sat up, trying not to put my hands on any frogs, and screamed again as I realized I had squished several with my body.

Nancy sympathetically began picking dead frogs off my back. As I got back up, I saw Frank grinning devilishly and Wanda giggling hysterically. I was beginning to feel a little bit hysterical myself. Mama walked in to start lunch but was stopped in her tracks by frogs trying to jump up on her, like tiny dogs greeting their master. She just stood there silently, looking grim. Milton happened on the scene and started scooping up the critters. "I name you Don, and you Bob, and you Tom, and you Rivet . . ."

Daddy walked in, scratching his head. "What on earth? It's the Egyptian plague of frogs! Where did all these things come from?"

Wanda managed to interrupt her giggling long enough to spill the beans. "Look at those two! Did you ever see anyone look so guilty? Haven't you seen them up there at the top of the ladder, staring into the water tank for hours every day? Marlyn and Nancy did it, Daddy!"

Daddy looked at us incredulously. "Why in the name of all the plagues of Egypt did you do such a thing?"

I looked down, chagrined, but when I chanced a glimpse of Daddy's face I saw just a hint of a smile in one corner of his mouth. "Well, you two," he said, trying hard to keep a straight face, "you were responsible for getting them in here, so you can be responsible for catching them and taking them back where you got them to start with."

"Have fun," said Frank. "You do know they're in the bathroom, too, and the bedrooms, all over the entire house!"

Frank was right. We started a canvass of the house, the best we could—I mean you practically couldn't walk down the hall without stepping on a frog. We found five of them in the toilet and a bunch more in the tub. And they were on our beds and in the kitchen drawers—I don't know how they got in the house to start with, let alone in all those places, but they did. Nancy and I thought we would never get them all caught, thrown into a covered bucket, and returned to the irrigation ditch, but eventually we did.

My next encounter with the local wildlife came one day when Wanda and I were running along a footpath, headed for home. Suddenly, mid-stride, I looked down and saw to my horror that my foot was just inches from landing smack on an enormous rattlesnake flicking its tongue, coiled and shaking its rattles, its mouth aimed up at my foot. Somehow my leg seemed to be lifted up away from the snake and brought down on the other side. I hopped away as fast as I could run up to Wanda, and frantically pulled her on down the path away from the snake.

Wanda was not unnerved by the snake the way I was. She was too busy thinking up what practical joke could be made of the experience. "Marlyn," she said excitedly, "let's tell Mama you got bit by a snake! It'll be the best April Fools' joke ever!"

I hesitated. "Wanda, I don't think that's such a good . . ." I began, but Wanda had begun to run ahead. Before I could catch up with her, I saw Mama running out of the house, stumbling in her haste, and heard Wanda call out, "April Fools'!"

Wanda was laughing, but it was no laughing matter. Mama had gone white and was shaking and sobbing. She looked as if she were about to fall over. "Wanda, come here and help me get Mama back inside the house," I said. The two of us piloted her into the house and to our parents' bedroom, where we helped her lie down on the bed.

"Get me a bowl," she said weakly. I grabbed a small decorative bowl off the dresser and stuck it under her chin just in time. "Querido Señor," I heard her whisper after she was done throwing up, "por favor ayúdame a criar esta niña sin que pierda la vida." ("Dear Lord, please help me to raise this child without getting her killed.")

Suddenly I saw what all my near-catastrophes had done to my mama. Over and over God had reached down and saved me from what looked like certain death. I was alive and well, but now Mama lived in fear about what might happen to me next. I had always known she loved me, but I'd never realized her love was this passionate. I felt simultaneously treasured and terrible.

By the time Daddy got home from work, Mama was much better, but Wanda and I were in deep trouble. The talk he gave to us that day was one of the sternest I have ever endured in my life. "Jokes cease to be funny when people get hurt, and your mother has been terribly hurt," he told us. "You saw how sick she was made by the fear she felt. She cannot bear the thought of losing any of her children. Promise me, both of you, that you will *never* try anything like that again. There will be consequences for what the two of you did."

"Daddy, please, no, it wasn't my idea, it was hers, and I tried . . ."

Beyond Ashes

"But, Marlyn, you *didn't* stop her, and that makes you as guilty as she is. I am sorry, but the two of you are getting the same punishment, because you both were a part of this." At the time I felt like I was being treated unfairly, but later on I came to realize it was a valuable lesson to learn—one I never forgot.

"Many times what we perceive as an error or failure is actually a gift. And eventually we find that lessons learned from that discouraging experience prove to be of great worth."[1]

---

1. Richelle E. Goodrich, *Smile Anyway* (CreateSpace, 2015), 33.

CHAPTER 5

"Mrs. Cardoza, I Want to Take You With Me"

It was my turn to clean the kitchen that week, and it looked sparkly clean. That afternoon, after working outside, Daddy walked into the kitchen. His eyes scanned the room. "Marlyn, when you clean the kitchen, I expect you to complete the task."

"But Daddy, I did finish . . ."

"Don't talk back to me, young lady! There are dishes that you haven't washed, and there are crumbs and food on the counter."

He moved toward me. Knowing I was innocent, I grasped his arm to stop him. "But Daddy, I did finish! That mess is not mine," and an argument ensued.

"What's going on here?" Mama entered the kitchen.

"Marlyn didn't finish cleaning the kitchen! She's denying it in spite of the clear evidence sitting there on the counter. I will not tolerate lying and backtalk. She must be disciplined!"

"Monrad—Marlyn finished her job. I came in and made a snack for myself before going to work. Those are my dishes and those are my crumbs." Mama spoke firmly.

Daddy's jaw dropped and his face fell. Without another word he left the kitchen. Shaken by the encounter, I gave a huge sigh of relief. I had thought I would be in so much trouble for resisting him!

Two hours later, Daddy found me alone in the living room. "Marlyn, please forgive me. I had no right to come at you like that. I should have listened to your explanation first." Then he folded his hands and looked heavenward. "Father, please forgive me for losing my temper with my daughter. You know I don't want to subject my children to my temper when I am tired. Please give me the victory, Lord."

I found myself wondering how many other fathers would have apologized to their daughters like that. Daddy indeed did lose his temper with one or another of us from time to time, usually when he was tired or stressed out, but he would always apologize and ask our forgiveness, and then pray out loud to ask God's forgiveness and help in overcoming his temper.

Best friends
Millie and Milton were three years apart, and pals. They, like me, were naturally inquisitive, always looking with fresh eyes at a world just waiting to be explored. We often gathered wildflowers and pretty rocks to take to Mama. They delighted in helping me beautify ant homes with little rocks and flowers. We would fill large bottle lids with water and create pools with tiny floating leaves.

Nancy and I often included my younger siblings in our outdoor fun. One of our favorite pastimes was playing pirates. We collected colorful pieces of broken glass for our treasure chest: our diamonds, rubies, and emeralds. A large contraption made of metal and wood sat on our property. It became our pretend ship to sail the high seas. We dressed as pirates. Milton and Millie were the rivals trying to steal our jewels. We captured them, loosely tied their hands with rope, and made them walk the plank.

Milton was curious and asked lots of questions. He was interested in my books and eager to learn. I read him character-building tales from *Uncle Arthur's Bedtime Stories*, and he never tired of hearing them. When Milton turned five, he asked me to teach him how to read. I borrowed a first-grade Dick-and-Jane reader from the school, and before long he was reading and writing, as well as working out simple math problems.

A new school
When Mr. Johnston, the new teacher for grades nine and ten, moved to Weimar, he was hired to drive the school bus. Now we had transportation to the school, and I was happy to be getting back into church school with my closest friends. About that time the school held a contest to rename the school. Daddy gave me the idea of Pine Hills Junior Academy. I submitted it and won a two-dollar prize.

Frank joins the navy
Shortly after turning eighteen, Frank left to join the navy. He seemed to

enjoy it, even boot camp. The navy made him a Radioman First Class and stationed him at the navy base camp in Okinawa, on the USS *Lexington* aircraft carrier. It seemed strange to have him gone, but he wrote lots of letters home, sometimes even accompanied by gifts.

First grade, eighth grade, at last!
When Milton turned six, Daddy announced that he could begin first grade in September. Each morning after that, Milton had looked with longing eyes as he watched his big sisters get ready for school. His cheery face would greet us when we arrived home from school, always with lots of questions.

A slight nip in the air signaled summer's end; school would be starting soon. Acorns crackled underfoot as we walked the dirt path to the bus stop. I had an extra spring in my step, because this year I was an elite eighth-grade student entitled to special privileges, including a class trip and graduation.

At the bus stop Milton's face glowed as I brushed his hair in the direction of the natural cowlick that swirled to the right above his forehead. Wanda rearranged the thick brown curls that draped to Millie's shoulders. At last we boarded the school bus, and the twelve-mile trip to the school began, with Mr. Johnston behind the wheel.

From time to time one encounters a young child so emotionally mature, so full of courage, so blessed with empathy and insight into spiritual matters, that it takes one's breath away. My little brother was such a child. I had often been amazed at his emotional and spiritual precocity; now I saw it even more clearly.

Sometimes after school I would venture over to Milton's classroom to chat with his teacher, Miss Lund. Her eyes sparkled as she described him as being the most eager of all her students. Smiling, she told how he would bend over the tales of Dick, Jane, and Sally and then vigorously waggle his arm in the air to answer her questions. New words were never a problem. He would figure them out quickly, ace the story assignment, then help the slower students. Whatever was going on, Milton was in on it, whether it was reciting memory verses, watercolor painting, or writing numbers to one hundred.

She related how during morning worship, Milton was one of the first children in the classroom to get up enough courage to come to the front

Beyond Ashes

of the room and offer prayer. When he led out in singing "In the Sweet By and By," or "When He Cometh," his voice and face showed his enthusiasm. I could tell by the glow on her face that he was teacher's pet. *I'm not surprised*, I thought.

Recess was always a refreshing change for the students to unwind from bookwork. The moment the bell would ring, we would rush out of our classrooms—first to the water taps and restrooms, and then to the open field, where tall pines looked like sentinels guarding the property.

During my afternoon recess break, I liked to glance over at Milton's class at play. He was always an exuberant participant, whether playing kickball or tag. One day I saw Milton do something involving the class half-pint and the class bully, which made my jaw drop. Billy, who came from a poor family with twelve children, was smaller than the other boys. Mac, who was bigger than the others, didn't always want to include Billy in the game, because he couldn't play as well as Mac thought he should. One day Mac shoved Billy, knocking him down. Milton immediately pounced on Mac and pinned him to the ground. He bent Mac's arm behind his back and in no uncertain terms informed him that he would not let him up until he promised never to pick on Billy again. When I saw this, I spontaneously glowed with big-sister pride.

As the days waned, autumn chilled the air. Summer's green gave way to fall's scarlet and gold. In just a few weeks the trees stood naked in the frozen air. We walked to the bus stop wearing warm hooded jackets and woolly mittens.

A new house on the hill

With the season of winter came two weeks of Christmas vacation and Christmas. Mama always made Christmas special. But this year was different. The California state highway system, as part of their plan to construct Interstate 80 all the way to Lake Tahoe, put up several motel units in Weimar to be sold at an auction. The state needed the land for the new interstate. Daddy was the only bidder and bought three at a very reasonable price, and in answer to prayer. He had them moved to the top of the hill on our property. The units were well-built, with hardwood floors and knotty pine walls, each having a large-sized bedroom and bathroom. He had the units placed so that the house would be in an L-shaped design. One bedroom would be on the shorter end of the L, and two bedrooms

"Mrs. Cardoza, I Want to Take You With Me"

would be on the longer end of it. With the help of a contractor, a large kitchen, living room, and dining room were built in the corner of the L between the bedrooms. They also added a front porch. Mama designed two large picture windows that overlooked a view of the Sierra Nevada mountains. Mama allowed Wanda and me to contribute in the interior decorating. We were excited about our new home, and that's where most of our activity was centered.

For Christmas, Daddy and Milton cut down a tree on our property, and we decorated it with homemade ornaments, popcorn, and candy canes. But gifts around the tree were slim pickings, because the new house, which couldn't be wrapped, was a Christmas gift for everyone. Daddy had hoped we could move in before Christmas, but inclement weather delayed things, and the move was postponed until the middle of January.

When school began again after Christmas, Miss Lund announced that since Milton was far ahead of the other students in reading, writing, and arithmetic skills, and already helping the second graders, she would like to pass him into second grade. Of course, Mama and Daddy approved. I had been his preschool teacher, and my heart was filled with pride for my little brother's achievements.

Mrs. Cardoza

In our neighborhood, Milton had taken an interest in an elderly woman by the name of Mrs. Cardoza. He volunteered to do her yard work, picking up kindling wood and stacking it so that she could burn it in her wood stove. He swept her front porch and shoveled snow in the winter. He also shared his love for Jesus by teaching her the Bible stories that he had learned from Daddy and from his church lesson guide, *Our Little Friend*. She loved to hear the stories.

One day he said to her, "Mrs. Cardoza, when I grow up to be a man, I'm going to be a missionary like my daddy. I want to take you along. We will go over the sea on a ship, and there we will buy a couple of donkeys. We will pile our suitcases on the donkeys and go over the hills and over the valleys to do missionary work for Jesus."

He paused. "But Mrs. Cardoza, I don't think I'll be able to take you along, because you smoke. Smoking is not good for you. You're going to have to quit smoking and start coming to church with me so that you can learn more about the Bible. Then you can go with me to the mission field." Mrs. Cardoza thought it was such a wonderful little talk, she told Mama all about it.

At home, during our family worship, Milton took the initiative in praying for the poor people, Mrs. Cardoza, and for the missionaries. If anyone left them out in their prayer, he'd remind them, "You didn't pray for the poor people, Mrs. Cardoza, and for the missionaries." Everyone in the family began to follow his example. The song Milton would always ask to sing was "When He Cometh." Milton was one of those precious jewels. Here are the lyrics for "When He Cometh":

When He cometh, when He cometh
To make up His jewels,
All His jewels, precious jewels,
His loved and His own.
Like the stars of the morning,
His bright crown adorning,
They shall shine in their beauty,
Bright gems for His crown.

He will gather, He will gather
The gems for His kingdom,
All the pure ones, all the bright ones,
His loved and His own. . . .
Little children, little children
Who love their Redeemer,
Are the jewels, precious jewels,
His loved and His own.[1]

---

1. W. O. Cushing, "When He Cometh," *The Seventh-day Adventist Hymnal* (Washington, DC: Review and Herald®, 1985), no. 218.

CHAPTER 6

"Marlyn, Don't Be Afraid"

A cold, biting wind penetrated my clothes as I opened the door of our new house. Daddy had just finished painting the front deck. "There's been a change in the weather. I'm going inside to catch the news."

"A cold front is moving in and expected to hang around for several days. It will be twenty-two degrees by nightfall," the weatherman's voice blared over the radio.

"Can you help me with the wood, Milton?" At the age of seven, Milton was already adept at cutting and stacking firewood. He and Daddy went back outside to cut up kindling wood, enough to fill the bin by the wood stove, then headed back outside.

"Marlyn, can you give me a hand with these larger pieces?"

Freezing air stung my face as I hurriedly stacked the wood in a neat row against the toolshed. Unbroken blackness loomed above—not a star in sight. As the porch light lit the darkness, Daddy reflected, "This shining light will serve as a watchtower to greet Mama when she comes home from work."

"Can't wait for Mama to see the bright new porch." Milton grinned, snapping the light off and on.

Millie shifted her eyes toward Daddy. "Yes, and we mustn't forget to leave the porch light on for Frank and Wanda." Frank had gone to Auburn, and Wanda was still at her boyfriend's house.

"For sure," Daddy replied.

Halfheartedly, I listened to family chitchat. Milton begged Millie to play a game of hide-and-seek. "Sure, Milton, but not for long; I want to color in my new coloring book."

"Remember, children, Mama likes to come home to a clean house," Daddy interjected. We hurried to do our chores.

Beyond Ashes

The green jacket

"Daddy, would you please clean my green jacket?" Milton asked.

"The one with a greasy spot this size?" Daddy gestured widely with his hands, a playful look in his eye.

"I'd like to wear it to school tomorrow, but I suppose I could wear the blue one. The green one is warmer, though, and *brrrr*, it's colder outside than the North Pole!"

"Milton, last week I promised to clean it for you, but I've been so busy I forgot. Sure, your daddy will clean it right now." Daddy put on a warm coat and went outside to the gasoline tank. Flashlight in hand, he poured a small amount into a can to use in cleaning the jacket. Milton watched from the outside doorway of the utility room.

Millie stood washing dishes at the kitchen sink, which was adjacent to the inside doorway of the utility room. I was in my room just off the kitchen, cramming for an English test. Unbuttoning my cardigan sweater to get ready for a shower, I heard a car drive up. It would be Mama coming home from work. Her footsteps pattered on the kitchen floor. I peeked out as she opened the utility room door.

"Monnie, I'm glad that you are cleaning Milton's jacket, but I've had an extra-hard day at work. I'm exhausted and I want to go to bed early. How long will it be before we can have worship?" Closing the door to my room, I buttoned the sweater back up in anticipation for worship. *I'll shower after worship.*

Suddenly—*BOOOOOM!* The house shook violently. I lurched back with a gasp, my hand shoved hard against my chest. An earthquake? A bomb? Terrified, I opened the door to see Millie streak by. "Help! Help! The house is on fire!" she screamed as she ran out the door into the darkness.

Mama, Daddy, and Milton appeared, looking like human torches. *A nightmare! Oh God, please, let it be a nightmare!* Flames engulfed the utility room—reality hit like a knife.

Daddy grabbed Mama's collar to pull off her coat. "Anita, unbutton your coat! You're on fire!" Mama unbuttoned her coat, and Daddy yanked it to the floor.

"Daddy, Daddy, I'm burning to death!" Daddy and Mama turned to help Milton. Mama used her hands to pat out the fire on Milton's hair. She ran out the door and down the road for help. I could see the energy

"Marlyn, Don't Be Afraid"

surging through Daddy's veins as he patted out the fire on Milton's clothes, simultaneously pushing him out to the porch and rolling him in a paint tarp lying on the deck. By now, giant crackling flames had reached the kitchen!

Panic-stricken, I sprinted outside. Part of Milton's pant leg was still burning, and Daddy pulled the pants off his legs. By the light of the fire I could see skin hanging from Daddy's hands. The nauseating odor of burning hair and flesh rolled over me in waves. Milton's hair had burned off, and his entire body appeared to be charred. I longed to gather him up in my arms. Gingerly, I touched the top of his head with my hand—it felt like a hot grilled steak. Quickly, I jerked it away!

Fear took over my body, and it shook with terror at the horror all around me. Milton looked up at me, his eyes reflecting the leaping flames. "Marlyn, don't be afraid." Calming strength came over me, but though I would try to be brave like Milton, I didn't know how to not be afraid.

"I'm feeling faint." Daddy eased himself to the ground.

Milton began to shiver. "Daddy, it's so cold. Let's go somewhere for help."

"Your daddy can't go any farther, but help will come. Marlyn, Mother has gone for help, and I'm sure she will be taken to the hospital. Run as fast as you can to the Johnstons' house. Ask Mr. Johnston to take Milton and me to the hospital."

Lifting my straight wool skirt above my knees, I took off into the night. "Oh, God! Help!" I cried again and again as I ran over chuckholes on the dirt road. It seemed my feet barely touched the ground. Pitch-blackness surrounded me, but up ahead, I could see the light of the McCalls' house, neighbors who lived a half-mile from our house. Looking back, I almost fell—our house was fully engulfed in giant flames, leaping and vaulting like a huge, malevolent beast. *Don't look back—aim for the light!*

Finally, I was there, pounding on the door. "Mr. McCall, our house is on fire! My parents and brother are terribly burned! Please take me to the Johnstons' house!" After a jerky high-speed drive down a tortuous road, we arrived at the Johnstons' house. Pounding on the door until a startled Mr. Johnston appeared in the doorway, I stammered, "My house is on fire! Mom, Dad, Milton—badly burned! Please, come quick!"

Jumping into Mr. Johnston's new 1957 Chevy station wagon, we took off, wheels flying over the curvy dirt road. Driving up the hill, we now saw the flames were high on both ends of our L-shaped house. Mr. Johnston cried out, "Oh my, there's no way we can save your house!"

We found Daddy and Milton sitting on the bank of the road. Milton's clothes had burned off, and his flesh was charred. Daddy's skin and part of his clothing hung off his arms and legs. After one look, Mr. Johnston yelled, "Get in! I'll take you to the hospital!"

I begged to go, but Daddy said, "No, you must stay by the house. Neighbors are arriving with blankets that will keep you warm, and you will be safe. Frank and Wanda will soon be home, and you must tell them what happened." Mr. Johnston pulled off.

A neighbor's car arrived with Mama and Millie inside. Millie had gone to his house for help. He told us that as they drove up the road, he had found Mama limping down the hill, clad only in a nylon uniform and trembling from cold and shock. When he saw that Daddy and Milton had found a way to the hospital, he speedily took Mama to the emergency room at Highland Hospital in Auburn. Millie rode in the car with them, comforting Mama as best she could. Millie told me later that Mama was in agonizing pain from the burns on her hands and legs. She had been wearing her nurse's uniform and white nylons under the wool coat that Daddy had taken off her. Her hands were badly burned from patting out Milton's fiery clothing, and her nylons had melted into her legs, burning them horribly. Her face had burns as well, but not a hair on her head had been touched by the flames!

Upon dropping Mama off, the neighbor took Millie to their house, where she would spend the night. I didn't see her again until the next morning.

Floorboarding it!
[This following section is adapted from Mr. Johnston's memoir, My Life Story.*]*
In about two miles, Mr. Johnston came to the new Interstate 80 freeway and "stepped on it"! Not seeing the California Highway Patrol (CHP) car in its usual hiding place, he "opened it up"—floorboarding it! In a mile or so he noticed headlights some distance behind, but they were getting farther back all the time. As he would later find out, it was the CHP car. It radioed ahead to the next patrol car near Auburn (about twelve miles away). "A car was high speeding by! I couldn't keep up well enough to read the license plate because it was going so fast! But it would have to be going more than 112 miles per hour!"

"Marlyn, Don't Be Afraid"

As Mr. Johnston neared the hospital and began to slow down, they passed the second patrol car, which turned on its red lights, but Mr. Johnston just figured it would follow him to the hospital and then they could talk. They could not keep up!

Daddy was crying out from pain. Looking over at him, Mr. Johnston saw that his skin was broken, hanging from his hands and body like the skin of a ripe tomato dropped into boiling water. He saw that all of Milton's clothing had been burned off and that his nerves must have been seared, because he obviously felt no pain.

"We'll be at the hospital soon, Daddy, and the doctors will make it so you don't hurt so bad," Milton said encouragingly as he hugged a blanket around himself. Soon they were at the hospital, where Mr. Johnston carried Milton to the emergency room. Then he came back and guided Daddy to the admission desk where he could take care of the paperwork.

The CHP car had indeed followed him to the hospital, and about fifteen minutes later, when he came out, he saw that the first patrol car had arrived also. They had opened the hood of the car to see what kind of engine he had! The officer was irate. He had been turning around behind the trees when he saw Mr. Johnston streak by. The officer claimed to have the fastest car between Sacramento and Reno, but he was losing ground to Mr. Johnston every mile until he was out of sight. The trooper was so mad he was swearing! He wrote up a ticket for 140 miles per hour. Later, when Mr. Johnston had to appear before the judge to pay for his traffic ticket of $140.00, Pastor Loewen and another church member, Ralph Sturgill, went with him to let the judge know this was an errand of mercy. The judge reduced the charge to $40.00, of which Ralph paid half.

At the hospital
[The rest of this account was given to me later by Mama, Daddy, and Gladys Estes.]
"Well, now that you're in good hands, I'd better go back to my kids—they're home alone." With that, Mr. Johnston was gone.

Daddy tried to ignore the agonizing pain long enough to fill out the forms thrust under his nose. "Ma'am, I can't quite see the print, it's swimming around on the page, and I can't pick up the pen; my fingers don't seem to work," he sobbed.

"No matter. Just give me your insurance card."

"I don't have it," he gasped. "It was in the house that burned."

"All right then, come this way, mister."

Daddy tried to do as ordered but found he couldn't stand up. A minute later an orderly arrived with a gurney and loaded him onto it, then wheeled him into a hallway in the ER. The ER personnel cut his clothes completely off and he was left, naked and freezing, for all to see.

"Nurse, nurse! Doctor! Anyone! Something for my pain! Please!"

His eyes were swelling shut, and he barely made out a face leaning over his. "You're at the county hospital! We can't treat you here!"

"Please! Just a shot! A doctor! I'll pay!" he shouted. "Anyone! Please!"

"Sir, please be quiet. You're bothering the other patients. You're not the only one back here, you know!"

He was shaking so hard with cold and shock that the gurney was actually bouncing around under him. Curious stares were thrown his way, but no doctor came, nor anything to lessen the unbearable torture. He felt rejected by man and forsaken of God.

"My God! My God! Why have You forsaken me?" Twice he repeated those words. Immediately, the thought came, *God would not leave me.* "Oh, God, relieve the pain in my body!" At once the prayer was answered. The torturous pain was relieved, and soon after that the ambulance arrived to take them to Highland Hospital.

On the short ride over, Milton was cheerful and talkative. "I hope the doctor gets me well in time for school tomorrow. Miss Lund will miss me if I'm not there." Then father and son were taken into surgery, and a merciful darkness swallowed them.

Weeping may endure for a night, but joy cometh in the morning
Gladys Estes, a registered nurse and friend of the family, arrived at the hospital to offer private duty care for Milton. He and her son Roger were good friends at school. After Milton's burns had been treated in surgery, she was told that over 85 percent of his body had third-degree burns and that he was not expected to make it through the night. As she sat by his bedside, he opened his eyes and asked how his daddy was.

Mrs. Estes said, "Milton, I want to pray for you and your daddy and leave everything to Jesus." After the prayer, together they hummed the words of Milton's favorite song. "When He cometh, when He cometh to make up His jewels, all His jewels, precious jewels, His loved and His own."[1]

"Marlyn, Don't Be Afraid"

Milton whispered, "Amen." And at one thirty in the morning a precious little lamb went to sleep in the arms of Jesus. His last words were, "Daddy, I'll see you in heaven!"

~~~~~~~

Dearest Milton
So often I've gone back to the night
You looked at me with eyes so bright.
So many times I've heard your voice,
"Don't be afraid"—it's now my choice.
If only I could've held your hand,
Kissed you gently to say you're grand.
And just before you had to go,
I wish I could've said, "I love you so."
I don't know how; I don't know why,
I had no chance to say goodbye.
Rest in peace, my little bro,
In the "morning," I'll tell you so.

---

1. Cushing, "When He Cometh."

CHAPTER 7

Torch on the Hill

Our house on the hill had become a torch that could be seen a mile away. People began to arrive, some of whom I hardly knew, and others whom I had never met. My eyes moved from face to face in the gathering crowd. People drifted around in a daze, not knowing what to say or do. As I stood in front of the inferno that was our house, I felt too numb to talk. A neighbor put a blanket around me. A pickup truck pulled up with my brother at the wheel. Frank ran toward the blazing house as though he were about to enter. Two men rushed up behind him and grabbed his arms. One man commanded, "Young man, don't go in there."

"My mom, my dad, my family—I've got to go in and save them!"

A man with a kindly face placed a hand on his shoulder. "Son, your mother, father, and little brother were badly burned and have been taken to Highland Hospital!" Staggering over to Frank with the blanket trailing behind, I tried to call out his name. Gagging in the smoke, only a raspy, barely audible sound came out.

Frank shouted over his shoulder as he darted to the truck, "I'm going to the hospital! I must see them!" In his haste to leave, I think he didn't see me.

Gusts of winter wind fanned the fire as it continued to rage, forcing me back. The flames produced eerie crackling sounds as they licked every inch of the house. Occasionally, explosions could be heard. Someone said, "It must be the gas cylinders of the house exploding under the pressure of the heat." Windows cracked and splintered; walls crumbled—in their place stood thick beams of charred wood. Soon they stood in the darkness like a skeleton. Just hours before, our home had been alive, vibrant. Inside had been a place of love and security, a place with memories and warmth. I shivered at the sound of wind whistling over the blackened wood and metal that had been furniture and appliances. In those ashes lay our photographs, our keepsakes, all our personal possessions. I felt weak and exhausted. I thought about my bed. I longed to crawl into it and pull the warm covers over my head. My mind drifted to the new bedspread with purple flowers that Mama had bought. *It's all a dream, all a dream, only a nightmare—a horrible nightmare! I'll wake up any minute now, just a dream, not real, not real!*

The piercing wail of a siren burst into my senses. Firefighters arrived, but too late to save the house. They sprayed the large propane gas tank that still stood next to the house. Grimly they watched the house burn into smoldering ashes.

I felt a gloved hand on my shoulder and a tender voice that I recognized. It was Peggy Johnston, our schoolteacher's wife. A thick winter jacket was draped over one arm, and in the other she carried a thermos with hot apple cider. I slipped into the jacket and sipped the hot drink that soothed my parched throat and warmed my insides. Peggy hugged me tight, and for the first time in what seemed an eternity, comfort flowed into my body.

"Wanda has been called. She knows about the fire, but I don't think she has been told about your parents and little brother. Her boyfriend, Donnie, is bringing her. I'll stay with you until she arrives. Then I'll take both of you to the hospital."

When my sister arrived I ran into her arms. Sobbing, we held each other. Peggy gently let her know that Mama, Daddy, and Milton had been burned and that they were being cared for in the hospital. Wanda gasped, raising a hand to cover her pounding heart as she took in the scene in front of her. Her face reflected the terror inside her body. Shaking, she sank into Donnie's arms, sobbing on his shoulder. He held her, stroking her hair.

At the hospital we were informed that our parents and Milton were in the burn unit and that we could not see them that night. A gurney rolled by with a small body entirely wrapped in bandages. "Your brother has just come out of surgery," a nurse informed us. Feeling faint, I sank into a waiting room chair. "It's standard procedure to wrap burn victims in bandages," she continued.

Wanda and I hugged each other. Oh to run, to go home, but we didn't have a home to go to—we were homeless. Peggy reached out and squeezed our hands. "You girls are coming home with me, and you can stay as long as you want."

Sorrow

The next morning I awoke to the sound of a doorbell ringing. Tucked under a warm blanket on a sofa bed, I sat up. But where was I? The doorbell rang again. Wanda, sleeping on her belly, rolled over and opened her eyes. Glancing toward the doorway, I watched as a figure clad in a blue bathrobe tiptoed to the front door. It was Peggy. Her husband, holding a piece of toast, peeked out from the kitchen doorway.

"Good morning, Myrtle. What brings you here so early?"

"I have sad news. The little boy didn't make it. Milton died at one thirty this morning." The events of the night before suddenly gut-punched me.

Peggy slowly bobbed her head up and down, giving herself a second to absorb what she had heard. Taking a step forward, she placed a hand on Myrtle's arm. "Myrtle, it was good of you to come, but the girls," she lifted a finger to her lips. "Wanda and Marlyn are in the living room sleeping on the sofa bed."

Myrtle gasped, "Oh, I'm sorry, Peggy. I didn't know they were staying with you. I feel so bad for them. Please know I want to help. Don't worry about cooking supper tonight. I will bring enough to feed all of you."

I shivered as waves of emotion swept over me trying to grasp the meaning of the words I had just heard. *Milton dead? My little brother dead?* The dreadful thought swelled as it pounded its way into my brain. *No! No! No!* I grappled with the blanket and pulled it tight up to my neck. Wanda went white clutching the blanket around her midsection and shuddered; her dark brown eyes grew wide.

Peggy knelt to the floor taking our fingers in her hands. "Girls, I want you to know you are not alone. We are here with you." Mr. Johnston was standing by her side. He rumpled her brown hair, and wrapped a stray curl around his finger, and nodded. Feeling as though my stomach had crawled up into my throat, I lay my head on Peggy's shoulder. So much was going on inside me, but I didn't know what to say.

Mr. Johnston was Wanda's teacher. He leaned forward, placing a hand on her shoulder and the other on mine. "I assure you, Peggy and I will be your second parents as long as you need us. There's no need for you girls to go to school today. You can stay here with Peggy." Glancing at his watch, he added, "I wish I could stay with you longer, but there will be students waiting to be picked up on my bus run. I must leave right away."

How well I knew the long bus route! A car trip to school under normal circumstances took about thirty minutes. But on the bus, with stops in Weimar, Eden Valley, Meadow Vista, and Auburn, it usually would take about an hour. How I loved that bus ride! I thought about my best friend, Darlene. We always sat together. Would she wonder why I wasn't on the bus? I thought about how we chattered and giggled most of the way to school. She knew all my secrets, and I knew hers. Sometimes Dale, who sat behind us, would teasingly poke us as he called us "Miss Fit" and "Miss Take." A part of me wanted to forget what had happened and to jump into the school bus, but I knew I couldn't. If only things could be as they had been!

The four Johnston children, Danny, Donnie, Dennis, and Lynda, had been eating breakfast at the kitchen table. Mr. Johnston walked into the kitchen. "Come, children, it's time to go." They grabbed their lunch boxes and boarded the bus that was parked under the trees in the driveway.

The telephone rang. After a few moments, Peggy hung up the phone. "It's Mrs. Stiles. She has offered to buy you some new clothes. We have arranged to meet at Rankin's clothing store in Auburn at around two this afternoon. From there, we will go to the hospital."

As I picked up my clothes lying on a chair in the living room, the smell sent my thoughts spiraling back to the events of the night before; I gagged. These clothes were all I owned. Perhaps new clothes would help.

Millie, who had spent the night with a neighbor, joined us around noon. As soon as she saw us, she fell sobbing into our arms. Wanda and I locked eyes over Millie's head and shook our heads no. The loss of her home, as well as having both parents in the hospital, was enough for her to deal with. No need to tell her right away about Milton. They were buddies. She would take it hard.

Peggy cupped Millie's tear-filled face in her hands. "You'll be staying with Lynda in her room." Lynda was Millie's best neighborhood friend. Millie looked up at Peggy, hugged her tightly, and smiled. Peggy gently dabbed away Millie's tears with a part of her apron.

"You girls be kind to yourselves. This is a difficult time for you" She paused. "I know your stomach must be tied in knots, but you have a long day ahead and you need nourishment. Cereal, milk, and fruit are on the table. If you can, please at least try a few bites. I have some calls to make, and then I'll be getting ready for the day. My house is your house. You gals help yourselves to anything you see."

There was a warmth and sincerity about Peggy that I had always admired. A secure feeling swept over me as I looked at this woman who had so kindly taken us in. I would try to eat for her, but then a stabbing pain hit my chest, and I practically choked on the banana. A few sips of orange juice helped to wash it down.

Hearing the sound of a car in the driveway, I peeked through the window. Nan Sturgill and her daughter Patsy climbed out of the car. Nan carried a basket of cinnamon rolls.

"These are warm just out of the oven. If you feel up to it, help yourselves."

My mouth watered even past the sick feeling in my stomach. I lifted a plump roll out of the basket. Wanda walked into the room, with Millie close behind. I picked out two and placed them into their hands. We savored a bite. Suddenly a sense of horror spread through me. What was going on with me? One moment life would seem normal and the next moment I would feel like I'd been smacked by a truck. My emotions reeled. Nan grabbed me and held me tight, and soon Wanda and Millie snuggled into the hug.

"Patsy is feeling so bad about what has happened that she doesn't feel like going to school today. She would like to spend some time with Millie, and I'd like to take her home with me for the day. That is, if it's all right with you, Peggy." Nan spoke with a friendly southern drawl.

"I'll be taking Wanda and Marlyn to the hospital to visit their parents, and Millie is under the age limit required by the hospital. I appreciate your offer, Nan. It's thoughtful of you, and I know she'll be in good hands."

Patsy, carrying her favorite doll, tucked it into Millie's arms. "This is for you. I want you to have it." Millie hugged the doll to her chest and turned a full circle while tears flowed down her cheeks. Arm in arm, Patsy and Millie walked out the front door to the car.

On the way to the hospital we stopped at Rankin's and bought pretty new clothes. I had no idea how to feel better, but I had to get a grip. I hoped that seeing me in something soft and pretty would make Mama feel a little better.

Beyond Ashes

Even though I walk
   through the darkest valley,
I will fear no evil,
   for you are with me;
your rod and your staff,
   they comfort me (Psalm 23:4, NIV).

CHAPTER 8

Could I Be in the Wrong Room?

Outside the window of Highland Hospital was a sea of flat rooftops under a thick leaden array of clouds. A familiar figure sat in the waiting room. Frank heaved himself up from a chair, propping his muscular frame against a post. Sheer exhaustion coated his washed-out face. I drew a deep breath. As his kid sister, I had so many times looked up to Frank as my big invincible brother. He was on home leave from the navy. Just two weeks before, Daddy had picked him up at the Greyhound bus station. When they pulled up the driveway, I thought how handsome he looked in his navy uniform, his cap cocked to his head, so strong, so confident. The navy had matured him.

My thoughts drifted back to when I was seven and Frank was thirteen. He hit a bluebird while riding his bicycle, and one of the wings appeared to be broken. Wrapping the injured bird carefully with his shirt, he carried it home in the basket of his bike. I watched him apply a sterile bandage on the outside of the broken wing and around the body under the healthy wing. He kept it in a box in his room and fed it insects and small pieces of fruit and berries. The bird did not survive. He held the dead bird in his hands. "I didn't mean to kill it! It flew right in front of me, but it's my fault it's dead." Tenderly he placed it in a small box and buried it in the ground. A cross made out of twigs marked its resting place.

These days Frank acted more macho most of the time, but I knew the tender side of him was still there.

Frank jammed his hands into his pockets and forced himself back against the upholstered seat, fighting to keep his usually proud face under wraps. He leaned against the seat, hooking an elbow across the back as he chewed on his lower lip to keep from crying. Nonetheless, pressing his face into his hands, he began to weep.

Unaccustomed to seeing her brother cry, Wanda touched Frank's

Beyond Ashes

arm. "I'm OK," a despairing sigh rose from deep inside. "Mom, Dad, Milton—it's my fault—if only I'd been there. Maybe it would've been me and not Milton." His voice trailed as he gazed through the glass doors. "Why wasn't it me? I'm the black sheep. Why Milton? He was the good boy," he gasped. I wanted to say something, but was dumbstruck.

Frank stroked his jawline with his thumb. "Are you girls here to see the folks?" We nodded. "Let me warn you, it's not going to be easy! It's bad—really bad." He gritted his teeth. A chill swept over me as I watched him wander to the window and stare.

The double doors in the corridor swung open as the pastor of our church approached, a calming presence in his bearing. "Wanda, Marlyn," he spoke gently. "How are you girls holding up?" My finger traced a pattern on my skirt. "I want you to know how deeply sorry I am about the loss of your little brother." A shockwave brought reality crashing in again. It was undeniable—Milton *was* gone. Milton, the best-natured child I had ever known—Milton, my little brother. I bit my lip, and my fingernails dug a crease into my palms.

"I can't begin to imagine your grief." The pastor cleared his throat and wiped his eyes with a handkerchief. "Please know that I care. I've just been to see your parents." He paused to wipe away a falling tear. "I regret to tell you, they are in very critical condition, especially your dad. Your brother's death on top of her physical wounds has hit your mother hard. She is grieving deeply. Your father is very weak and under heavy sedation and has not been told. Your mom is awake and has asked to see you. She needs to know you are all right. The doctor thinks that it would boost your parents' recovery if they could see you for at least a minute or two." His eyes were kind. "You girls are so young. I look at you as though you were my own daughters. I wish I could spare you from any more pain than you've already been through, but it's going to be a long, hard road for your family. Your parents need your support. Are you up to visiting them?" I nodded, grabbing at my skirt and pulling hard.

"I'll go with you." Peggy held out her hands.

"Lord, I ask for Your comforting presence to be with these girls as they visit their mom and dad. Give them the strength and the faith they need at this most difficult time of trial." We bowed our heads as Pastor Loewen petitioned God.

Faith—this word I had grown up with seemed incomprehensible.

Could I Be in the Wrong Room?

Why did God allow my little brother to die so young? How could I—how could any of us live without him? And why did He allow my parents to be so badly burned? These were the first of many questions I would ask God.

A nurse, looking worn-out and stressed, led us down the long sterile-looking hall to the burn unit. A white cap bobbed atop her high-piled hair. "Your father has just awakened. You can only stay a minute. Then I'll take you to your mother's room. Your parents are badly burned. It's not a pretty sight. Your coming will mean a lot, though, and I'm right here if you need me."

Daddy lay propped on pillows in his bed, tubes protruding from all parts of his body. His face was enormously swollen, his neck so distended that it was even with his chin and jawline. His eyes were swollen shut. Ooze seeped through the bandages that covered his head and neck.

Tremors wrenched my insides. I was incredulous. *Could I be in the wrong room?*

Daddy barely whispered our names. *No—it's real.* Chills raced down my spine. It seemed a nightmare. Screaming, running would have brought relief. On the outside, I remained calm—for Daddy's sake. On the inside, pain—deep to the core pain.

Could he hear my heart pounding? *Be strong. Daddy needs me. He must not die.* My sister stood next to me. Immersed in each other's pain, we shared an emotional bond that we had never experienced before. The man lying there in that bed, with a monstrous face, swollen beyond recognition, was our daddy. For his sake we had to endure.

"Daddy, you are strong. You've always taught us to be strong. You are going to make it." The muted words came softly from my lips. Wanda nodded. A surge of strength flowed through me. God was in that room. The weakness of my faith didn't matter. He was there. He was giving me strength.

The nurse beckoned, "Follow me to your mom."

Mama's face was swollen, but her head was free of bandages. A cradle made of sheets covered her body, holding them off her burns. "My girls, my girls," she moaned.

"How is my Millie?" she wanted to know. Then, "Oh my little Milton," she began to sob. "I can't bear it—he's gone. He's gone."

"Nurse, my hands, my legs are hurting. Please, another shot." Her mouth quivered.

Beyond Ashes

"Your mom needs to rest." The nurse ushered us out.

In the hallway, Peggy wrapped her arms around our waists. "I don't mean to take your mom's place. I know what it is to miss someone you love and I know you will, but I want you to know you are not alone—I am here with you." She held and squeezed us hard. *I must be strong. I must not cry.* I bit my lip and dug my fingernails into my palms, a means of survival.

Every day for the next two months, Peggy drove us to visit our parents. On school days, she picked us up after school. It was painfully hard, especially in the beginning, but we wanted our parents to know we would be there for them.

Recovery

During my parents' slow convalescence, careful nursing and physical therapy gradually restored them to health. The medical professionals cared for them day after day, pouring their whole hearts into everything they did. My parents' vital signs were checked hourly. Changing their bandages, an excruciating ordeal, had to be done at least once a day and took two hours. Without that minute-by-minute care, my parents would never have survived.

The oozing I saw when visiting my dad was due to the fact that third-degree burns cause fluid to be released from the body's blood vessels. This can prevent the body's organs from receiving the amount of nutrients they need. As a result, Mom and Dad received intravenous fluids that gave their bodies the energy needed to function and to heal before and after the necessary skin grafts.

It was a miracle that Mama's face and hair had not caught on fire. Mama had second- and third-degree burns on her hands and legs that would require skin grafting. During the skin graft, a piece of healthy, unburned skin was surgically removed from her thighs and/or abdomen to cover the burned areas. After the skin grafting, the dressings covering their burn injuries had to be changed regularly. Their wounds were examined regularly to ensure that the graft would adhere to their skin and that it would heal properly without infection.

One reality that was hard for me to accept was the up-and-down pattern of their recovery. I'd be ecstatic at seeing a wonderful improvement in their spirits or the healing of their skin, only to be distraught the next

Could I Be in the Wrong Room?

day when all the progress seemed to be erased. Eventually I came to understand that this is par for the course with burn patients.

The day came when the doctor told us that Dad's recovery was no longer in doubt. He was still weak, still in pain, but our dad would not be leaving us anytime soon! Of course, Mama's recovery had never been in doubt, something for which I was and am extremely grateful!

Mama and Daddy, I wish you well a hundred times a day in my heart.

CHAPTER 9

Would Spring Ever Come Again?

Death had never been a fear of mine until now. I never ever wanted to make anyone cry, and seeing how Milton's death had affected my mother, from that point on I wanted to be brave, to be strong for Mama. I knew in my heart that Daddy would survive. He was always strong—but Mama? It would be harder for her.

The second day after visiting them in the hospital, Peggy parked the car in the driveway of our home. Fresh crisp air kissed my face. A leap and a sprint, feet crunching through piles of dead leaves, and I arrived at the big oak tree—my haven! The thick trunk, like a bodyguard, had always protected me from bullets I imagined would fly toward my body—a place to escape to when my older siblings and I were in battle. I looked at the branches—my fort. No one else could climb as high as I could. But this time, I leaned against the hardness of the bark—something sturdy.

Winter had stripped the tree of its innocence. It bore the naked truth; my little brother was dead like the withered leaves—Milton, who was my ally. I longed to hear his footsteps. I longed to hear his voice. *Would spring ever come again?* I wondered.

For me, the worst part of grieving is the time from the second of the death notification until the funeral. During that time there is no closure, no celebration: just sadness, pervasive sadness. For three days I sat, wooden. Nothing felt right. At school, each class was unbearably long. At recess, my best friend, Darlene, sat with me in the grassy field. She understood my need for quietness. She was there—that's all I knew. Silently I questioned, *Why God, why did You take Milton away so soon in life?* I could only wait for the funeral to come. Then would hell be over?

Precious jewels, His loved and His own
I stepped quietly into the Chapel of the Hills, slowly, tentatively, dreading

what I was about to see. Black-suited attendants escorted Wanda, Millie, and me to the family room, where we joined a few other family members. Through the window we could see people filing in. Many were children. Chairs were set in the hallway. It was a big funeral, a very big funeral for one little boy. Milton, wearing a white shirt and dark tie, lay undisturbed, untroubled in a white casket. I struggled to accept the thought that this would be the last time I would see my little brother for the rest of my life. Hymns played softly by the organist cast a peaceful ambience. Miss Lund sang: "When He cometh, when He cometh to make up His jewels, all His jewels, precious jewels, His loved and His own . . ."[1]

Tears flowed freely. Milton was one of those precious jewels, so much loved and so much in the hearts of the people.

Funerals are designed to bring closure to loved ones, but all I felt was pain. My stomach sank, and I blocked out most of the funeral service. I expected to cry, to let all the pain out in one blow. Yet I didn't cry much. I felt cold, numb, as if I, too, had died. Looking at my brother for the last time, I said goodbye to a piece of me. I tried not to look at him. I didn't want to come to grips with the fact that he was gone. The strange thing was that it brought out a sheer delusion—a vision of him by my side, snuggling up to me, whispering my name. It was a delusion I didn't want to lose.

The last memory I have of the funeral is Milton's casket being lowered into the grave. I now knew I could not get him back. I would never get him back. But how could he be gone? He was still wrapped around me in every step I took. Milton's free spirit and exuberance could not be taken away, for they were locked inside my heart. Some things in life cannot be repaired; they can only be carried. That, I could do. I could *carry his memory forever*. That's what the preacher had said.

God, where are You?

I was left with a pervasive survivor's guilt that haunted me for many years. *Why did God allow Milton to die? Why did God save my life so many times, especially in that hole in Mexico? And why did He not save Milton? Why him? Why not me?* This guilt became the genesis of my hiding from the truth I once knew. It became my self-sabotage—my brokenness. Would I ever trust God again?

Throughout my teenage years after that horrific night, my pain never

Would Spring Ever Come Again?

became completely eradicated. I just learned to channel it into staying active, into becoming an achiever at school, and into being there for Mama, for Millie, and for Daddy when they needed me. Actually, not so much Daddy; he was a man of faith—a faith I admired. A faith I once had. *Would I ever have that kind of faith again? Could I be brave on my own?* I could smile through my pain. I could pretend it didn't happen.

I sensed maybe God was there. Maybe He would not deny me my humanness. Maybe He would not deny me the right to rant, to rave, to question. I can't rightfully say I made it through simply because I was strong enough; that I became "successful" because I "took responsibility." To deny that God was there would be to deny God. I stood at the intersection of my greatest fragility and despair—so many uncertainties. *God, where are You? In spite of my apathy—are You there?*

God was in people
God's love was reflected through Peggy, who offered us a "Mom" relationship. We survived—we lived—because she chose to love us. She loved us in her silence, in her tears, in her willingness to suffer alongside us. She loved us in her willingness to be as pain-wracked, as destroyed as we were. She gave us the best gift she could offer: she gave herself not only for an hour, a week, or a month, but for the two months she daily drove Wanda and me the twelve miles to the hospital to visit our parents. She stood by our side at their bedside. She held our hands. She hugged us. She loved us. She took us into her heart and home as though we were her very own. Love was personified in Peggy.

God's love was reflected through Mr. Johnston, who offered us a "Pop" relationship. He helped us to see that going to school and being with friends was better than being alone and mourning. On Saturday nights he made chocolate fudge and popcorn. He kept our now "big family" of seven children active, sometimes playing Ping-Pong, Rook, or table games on the dining room table, or playing outdoor games. He loved us with lighthearted laughter, gentle teasing, and jokes. He provided us with chores, such as helping his son Donnie care for and milk the cows—a disaster at times, but no matter. He solved problems—one bathroom, nine people? No problem. He took the lock off the bathroom door and designed an "Occupied" sign to be strung to the doorknob for bathroom activity. Three extra daughters? No problem—mirrors were hung around the house for grooming. He allowed Wanda's boyfriend, Donnie, to visit her regularly. Mr. Johnston was Wanda's ninth-grade teacher. Did he lighten up on her? No, like a true papa he made her study. He made us all study.

A relationship is more important than reason. Healing is found when we have others who are willing to enter that space alongside us. The Johnstons entered that space and became our second parents. They remained forever "Mom and Pop Johnston" until they entered their rest within a year of each other, after each had a difficult bout with cancer. We look forward to renewing our bond with them in the sweet by and by, in the land of no more sorrow, no more death—our eternal home.

Day by day, life went on. At times my ability to function well was reduced. When needed, I allowed myself to cocoon, to cry heart-wrenching sobs from the depths of my soul. I didn't know how to acknowledge it at the time, but the Creator of all things beautiful was there to share tokens of His love. In the spring came the arrival of new life—little buds—vibrant leaves. The tree offered shelter. It offered comfort. It offered hope.

> *"Drinking from the waters of sorrow sustains a different kind of life. This river is hidden from the rest of the world. Tears drip off my chin into an endless flow of liquid love that sparkles with beauty."*[2]

Daddy's hands

Daddy's condition was critical. For the first part of his hospital stay he remained continuously under the skilled care of volunteer nurses from the church. It was a day-by-day process with no given hope that he would live. Because of the severity of his condition, Dr. Kindopp delayed in telling him about Milton's passing, because he knew it would affect him gravely, imperiling his recovery even further. When it appeared that Daddy had cleared the first hurdle of escape from death, the doctor decided he couldn't prolong the painful news, the kind of news doctors dread to tell their patients.

"I have sad news for you, Brother Olsen. I'm sorry to tell you that your little boy didn't make it." He spoke with compassion in his voice and tried to remain composed.

Daddy stared in disbelief. He recalled that when he had arrived at the hospital, he had said to the doctor, "My hands are badly burned, but I

Would Spring Ever Come Again?

saved my boy's life." This bright thread running through his mind was what had helped him endure the agonizing pain. Not once had it occurred to him that Milton might not make it. The doctor's news was just too much to swallow. Tears poured down Daddy's cheeks as he looked at his bandaged hands, too choked to speak.

"Brother Olsen, this is clearly terrible news that I have given you. I can't imagine what you're going through." The doctor paused. "Please know that I care and that I'm just around the corner if you need me." The doctor stayed by his bedside for a few moments and then left, gulping back some of his own tears.

Daddy was devastated. He looked toward the ceiling. "Why, God? Milton blossomed like a sunflower for almost seven years. Now, for no reason I can understand, he is gone—my beloved son is gone." Daddy began to tremble from shock. An icy cold chill came over him, and he felt as though his life were dangling on a string.

"Milton didn't make it. There's no point in living," he moaned. "How peaceful it would be to go to sleep and not wake up again." Startled by what he was thinking, he brought visual images of Mama and each one of his children to his mind. "No—no—I must make it! I have to make it! But I feel that my very life is ebbing out of me." He spoke out loud and rang for the doctor.

"Doctor, I'm so cold I'm shivering. Am I going to make it?" The doctor turned to the nurse and ordered warm saline dextrose into the vein. Daddy felt better and asked for a hot drink. The nurse brought him a cup of hot Postum, which warmed him up. For the first time since he had arrived, he didn't feel nauseous.

The next day, more terrible news came when the doctor informed Daddy that the nerves and blood vessels in his hands had been so badly damaged that he would never be able to use them again. This news, on top of everything else, seemed more than Daddy could bear. What would become of him now? Was there even any reason for him to go on living?

Turning his face to the wall, he reflected. *I've lost Milton. I am utterly helpless without the use of my hands—I'll be a burden. I've lost the dream house I built for my family. I'm worthless. What's the use of going on? What a relief it would be to be in no more pain! Wouldn't it be easier to die? God, let me die! I can't take it anymore. Please end this suffering!* he begged.

As Daddy lay there trembling, his eighteen years of mission service

Beyond Ashes

in Mexico flashed before his mind. He recalled the innumerable times God had delivered him from what seemed like certain death. He thought about how God had brought him through malaria and blackwater fever. He remembered how he had been stung by the deadly bark scorpion and how Indians had buried his body in the dirt to draw out the venom and save his life. He thought about Mama and each one of his children.

I still have Anita, Frank, Wanda, Marlyn, and Mildred! I can't die! They need me! Lifting his face heavenward, Daddy cried out, "O God, my wife, my children need me! I need the use of my hands. *Please heal my hands!*" Suddenly, the room filled with a glowing light. He saw heavenly angels all about him. For the first time since the fire, he felt movement in his hands—a tingling sensation! An enormous peace flooded over him. He knew that God had answered his prayer!

Ringing for the doctor, he pleaded, "Doctor, please take the bandages off my hands! You're going to be in for a surprise!"

"Well now, let's see." Dr. Kindopp carefully removed the bandages. His eyes grew wide in astonishment!

"Brother Olsen, the skin is growing back—your hands—why, your hands are healing! This indeed is a miracle!"

That evening, when we came to visit Daddy, we noticed a change had come over him. He told us how his hands had been healed, and we rejoiced together. Our visit was deeply meaningful. In all future visits, no matter what he was going through, no matter what depression snagged him, we were able to provoke a smile and good humor. Within six weeks, after treatments and physical therapy, Daddy regained full use of his hands. He would always carry the scars, but he wore them bravely as a reminder of how God had healed his hands.

"My health may fail, and my spirit may grow weak, but God remains the strength of my heart; he is mine forever" (Psalm 73:26, NLT).

---

1. Cushing, "When He Cometh."
2. Todd Nigro, "Thoughts on Grief and Loss," Ellie's Way, http://elliesway.org/thoughtsongrief/.

CHAPTER 10

Homecoming!

I'll never forget the day our parents came home from the hospital. Sunlight cast a glow on the cedars that lined the driveway. Familiar pine trees waved friendly hellos. But the best was yet to come—*a surprise waited inside.* Church members had renovated our one-hundred-year-old farmhouse, restoring it to former glory. The old farmhouse, with new cosmetic surgery, was set to rock again.

Friends from the church shepherded Mama and Daddy in wheelchairs through the kitchen. Spring flowers in vases perfumed the air, accentuating the delicate yellow hue on freshly painted walls. Wallpaper with tiny pink flowers transformed the walls of the dining room. Cushions on the chairs around the table that had hosted family and friends were adorned with burgundy and pink stripes. Each chair beamed an inviting welcome.

The living room displayed a brand-new two-piece sofa set with an area rug under the coffee table. The rooms in the house were coordinated with lamps, accessories, pictures, bedding, towels, and dishes suitable to each room. Clothing filled the closets; some new, some used. The cupboards and refrigerator were stocked with food, and freshly baked bread complemented a sumptuous home-cooked meal, ready to be served. The house sparkled with the handiwork of men and women who had spent days and weeks of detailed remodeling and decorating.

The icing on the cake came when Daddy was handed an envelope containing a message that the Community Services from a variety of Adventist churches throughout California, as well as the local church, had devoted sufficient funds to take care of our family's financial needs until we could get back on our feet. Overcome with gratitude for the love so incredibly lavished, their eyes flooded with tears, and they could hardly speak. It was a spectacular homecoming!

The power of grace is nowhere as radiant as in communities of faith.

Beyond Ashes

Its power includes coming together and showing that love is real. We were in such an atmosphere. Our family was bathed in healing love.

Learning to adapt

Returning to the old homestead was a welcome change, but nonetheless difficult; like taking a first breath after nearly drowning. I felt like an outsider looking at the puzzle of life around me. Once that life had been normal; now the pieces no longer fit. My finger traced a line on the wall that showed Milton's last growth spurt. His picture on the fireplace mantel smiled at me, with the same bright eyes I had last seen in the glow of the fire—eyes that said, *"Marlyn, don't be afraid."* A tear trickled down my cheek: like Milton—I must be brave.

I remembered the words Daddy once said, "Resistance to life's changes means cessation to live. There is power in positive thinking. Choose life!" Were my problems bigger than I was? Smiling back at the picture, I vowed that no matter how depressing and bleak my life looked, I could learn to adapt. There were hurts, lots of them, but I must look and find things that were good. In an effort to remain positive, I tried not to think about the fire. I tucked the pain deep into my subconscious. But grief cannot be tucked away. Always there are aftershocks: memories—reminders. When these would come, I'd run to my oak tree—my place of refuge. In the strength and solitude of its branches, I could sob.

Getting back up

It's one thing to develop nostalgia for home. It's something else to go home after a long hospital convalescence. Wanda and I had participated in a training session for a follow-up home program. We were told that the skin tissue that had been grafted had the potential to become very tight, which could severely restrict the range of motion needed for functional activities. We learned how to give soft-tissue massage and how to apply pressure wraps to assist with edema reduction. Physical therapists assisted Mama and Daddy in regaining the strength, endurance, and balance needed for activities such as getting into a chair, standing, and walking. Range-of-motion and stretching exercises were prescribed. Occupational therapists prepared them to resume the daily living skills of bathing, dressing, hygiene, and grooming. Outpatient therapy sessions were provided to prepare them to return to their employment. We

Homecoming!

learned that recovery could take up to as much as a year and that our full participation in the rehabilitation process was essential.

"Your parents are hard-working patients. They put in a great deal of effort and never complain. We can assure you that working together as a family, and with the aid of the team, the outcome will be success."

The wait to have our parents home again had been protracted. They had come a long way since that horrific night, but we knew they still had a long road ahead. At times upbeat and spunky, at other times the opposite, their ability to overcome huge obstacles defined their character. To get back up when life grinds you to the dust was a lesson they modeled, one we never forgot. During school hours, caregiving friends came over to assist with routine needs. After school hours, Wanda and I juggled parent care with household chores.

The school year came to a close. I had thought that summer would bring a welcome relief from the endless churn of school and homework mixed with housework and parent care. Instead, buried emotions came back to life, and I found myself once more lost in a morass of grief. Children and teenagers express emotional distress differently than adults do, simply because they often have a smaller frame of reference for how they feel or have less ability to effectively communicate how they feel. With the busyness, I had put grieving on the back burner. Given the circumstances, I thought I was OK. A major factor that had allowed me to be OK was school, classwork, and being with friends. Now that school was out for the summer, I had more time to think about what had happened. Yesterday I thought I was doing OK. Today my reality was different. Today I must navigate the ever-lingering darkness. I could not cast the pain out of my life, though I wanted to. My brother's memory haunted me, touching everything I did.

City adventure

A splendid surprise popped up when Aunt Alice, Daddy's sister, came for a visit. I was ecstatic when she invited me to spend a month of summer vacation with her—even more so when Daddy allowed me to go. She and Uncle Ralph lived in Van Nuys, a suburb of Los Angeles. The neighborhood, with neatly manicured subdivisions, was poles apart from country life, but I reveled in the diversity. Aunt Alice's soothing voice calmed my spirit. She was my dad's kid sister, and I loved hearing stories about how they grew up on a farm in South Dakota. When she described prairie life,

Beyond Ashes

I imagined a gigantic sea of grass feeding hundreds of farm animals and wild horses. I could picture neat rows of corn and potatoes waving in the breeze. But the sod house they grew up in—shelter to a family with eight children—was harder for me to wrap my mind around. I had a hard time visualizing a house made out of squares of piled grass.

"Your dad was an amazing equestrian, lassoing and training wild horses. I was six years old when he taught me how to ride my first horse." Adoration was in my aunt's voice when she spoke of Daddy.

Aunt Alice was affectionate and loving. In her presence I felt safe and relaxed. A middle child at home, I now basked in the warmth of being an only child, created just the boost I needed. Frequent forays around the area and getting acquainted with Norwegian cousins hyped the adventure. It was, in the lingo of the late-fifties, groovy to spend time with my cousin Ruby and her husband, George, who was fun-loving and a big tease. He spoke with a delightful Czechoslovakian accent and was as handsome as my cousin was beautiful. George worked in film colorization for Warner Brothers Studios in Hollywood. Because of his connections, he was able to make special reservations for us to dine at the Bistro Garden Restaurant in Beverly Hills. The restaurant was elegant, flaunting marble floors and palatial chandeliers. It provided sophisticated dining for the beautiful people of the world: royalty, movie stars, and high society. Though the menu offered elegant food selections, I settled on an incredible fruit salad.

The maître d' of the restaurant walked past our table, escorting the most handsome man I had ever seen in my life. "That's movie actor Ty Hardin," Ruby whispered. "Warner Brothers just contracted him for the TV show *Bronco*." I watched spellbound as the host seated him at a nearby table. Putting on my best manners, I pretended to be a princess, but alas, he didn't look my way.

"Daddy, how come you are so pretty?"
I enjoyed my stay with Aunt Alice, and the month went by far too quickly. When I returned home, Wanda was leaving to spend a month's vacation with her best friend, Jean, who had recently moved near the campus of Pacific Union College (PUC). Wanda enjoyed her getaway. When Jean's mother invited her to live with them and attend PUC Preparatory School for tenth grade, Mama and Daddy thought it would be a good opportunity and gave their approval.

Homecoming!

Soon the new school year was in session. Our parents had recovered to the point where they could stay home alone while Millie and I were in school. A nurse friend of Mama's would stop by for a daily check-up. Mr. Johnston, now my ninth-grade teacher, provided time for me to get my schoolwork done during study hall. That way I could help out at home.

With Wanda away, I moved up in the pecking order and assumed the role of oldest child. Millie and I shared parent care and household chores. Each of us carried a void in our hearts for Milton, and we clung to each other for support. Millie took to nursing like a duck takes to water and promptly picked up on ways to help with Mama and Daddy's care. Whatever they needed, she would be quick to fetch.

The left side of Daddy's face was scarred with a discolored raised area described as keloids. The pinna (narrow outer part of his left ear) had burned off. When Daddy was unhappy about how he looked, Millie would cup his face in her hands and say, "Daddy, how come you are so pretty?"—something she had started as a little girl when he appeared to be down in the dumps.

He would say, "My precious little daughter, thank you. Your daddy needed that!" Always eager to please, Millie was the apple of Daddy's eye.

Grief and recovery

Millie and I shared the same bedroom. Together we trembled, for we had had a run-in with pitch-black darkness, and we lived in fear of it now, so we slept with the light on. Sometimes she would have a nightmare, experiencing a recurrence of that dreadful night, and she would wake up screaming. I would hold her hand and sing her favorite songs until she fell asleep again. And so life went on.

Daddy traversed the bumpy valleys of the grief cycle with the normal human reactions of shock, numbness, denial, guilt, depression, and searching. At times he blamed himself. If only he had remembered to clean Milton's jacket before the cold front had moved in! If only he had been more aware of the explosive nature of gasoline! As he gave God his despairing thoughts, his eyes saw his faults. He looked again. His faith saw his Savior. It was too late to pull out the mistake. He let it go, and he was free.

Mama grieved heavily the loss of Milton. Grief was draining, sometimes exhausting, and she fell into a deep depression. One day after school I found her in the bedroom, packing a suitcase.

Beyond Ashes

"Mama, what's going on?"

"I must get away—too many memories in this house. Everywhere I turn I think of Milton. I can't bear it." She sat down on her suitcase and began to weep.

"Where would you go?"

"To Grandma Edith's."

"No, Mama, please, you must not go. I've lost Milton. I can't lose you too. If you go, I'll go with you."

"No, you must stay here and go to school. You must look out for your daddy and little Millie. You are strong—they need you."

"Mi preciosa Mamacita, Daddy and Millie need you. I need you. Por favor, no se vaya." ("Please, don't go.") I knelt on the floor, buried my head in her lap, and sobbed. Soon Mama got up and unpacked her suitcase. I guided her to bed. While she rested, I massaged her head and then her feet. As I sang her favorite song, "His Eye Is on the Sparrow," she hummed while I sang. The next day the doctor prescribed medication that helped Mama get through the crisis.

As Mama and Daddy searched over what had happened, they acknowledged that God's ways in allowing the tragedy were beyond their understanding. Daddy reasoned that to say that God was present in the tragedy did not mean that He made the event of the fire happen. Instead, it happened under its own volition, as arbitrary as a volcanic eruption. As their faith strengthened, they moved toward trusting God in a deeper way. God gave them new life, renewed hope, physical healing, and peace beyond understanding. When they came to the point of enjoying the fruit of recovery, it was like a dream come true. Laughter came back into our home. Humor and music lifted our spirits. In time we began to appreciate the good things that had happened, especially the miracles. Joy began to be the norm again. The sad things would always remain a part of us, but the happy and gracious things would too.

> The LORD is a refuge for the oppressed,
>   a stronghold in times of trouble.
> Those who know your name trust in you,
>   for you, LORD, have never forsaken those who seek you (Psalm 9:9, 10, NIV).

CHAPTER 11

"I Don't Know What Else It Could Have Been!"

At long last Mama and Daddy were not only walking without canes but were able to do such things as showering, managing buttons, and even some cooking on their own! I had hoped for this day but had not allowed myself to believe in it for fear of being disappointed. I still did the heavy housework, but they were now in charge of their own personal care and did light housework.

I knew the worst was definitely behind us when I heard them talking about a trip to Mexico.

"Wouldn't it be great to see everyone again? We could get ourselves a decent car and rent a trailer to tow behind us."

"Do you think you could actually manage the driving? You remember what the roads were like, don't you? And the traffic! You know your hands are still not quite what they were before the fire."

"Well—too bad Frank is in the navy. Do you suppose Wanda could manage the driving?"

I had my doubts about this last idea. Actually, the whole idea had a pie-in-the-sky quality to it. But it was so good to hear them talking about having fun again!

Next thing I knew, Wanda was taking driving lessons from her boyfriend, Donnie. They managed to scrounge up an old trailer from somewhere to practice with, and the two of them took to going off on minor excursions around the neighborhood: Wanda at the wheel, Donnie by her side occasionally reaching over to correct the angle of the steering wheel. The trailer tagged amiably behind. I had to admit, Wanda did amazingly well!

Mama started making lists of things to do and take. Meanwhile,

Beyond Ashes

Daddy began hunting for a suitable car: one strong enough to pull a trailer, dependable enough not to break down on a serpentine mountain road, and cheap enough that we could afford it. He ended up with a 1955 Mercury—it was aqua green with a white top. Now we needed a trailer where we could eat our meals and sleep at night. He wound up renting a trailer big enough to sleep all five of us.

Finally the trailer was loaded and we were ready to go. We climbed into the car with Wanda at the wheel, Daddy sitting beside her, and in the back Mama and me with Millie in the middle.

Day one lay through California, day two through southern Arizona. Let me tell you, southern Arizona in July is hot, hot, and hot! This was before the days when cars had AC, remember! We rode with the windows down, the hot dry air whipping our hair around our faces. Finally, on day three, we entered Mexico at Nogales.

For much of the way, the road through the Sonoran Desert lay straight as a carpenter's plumb line, mile upon mile with neither traffic nor gas station. From time to time Daddy would take the wheel to give Wanda a rest. And whenever we did actually come upon a gas station, we stopped and fueled up.

The final leg of the way to Mazatlán lay along the coast. I had vague memories of the west coast of Mexico from our train trip when I was three years old. Then it had been coast on the left-hand side and mountains on the right. Now it was reversed, with coast on the right and mountains on the left.

Finally we were at our first stop in Mexico—Mazatlán! Wanda eased the trailer into a berth at a trailer park, and we all swarmed into the trailer, pulling swimming gear out of drawers and finding spots in the trailer where we could change. Then down to the water. The aquamarine water was clear as glass, but shimmered as glass could not. Resting lightly on its surface, you could look down and see your shadow on the sandy floor of the bay. Mama dived down to the bottom and burst back above the surface into Daddy's arms, laughing. I felt like weeping for joy.

After two days of playing in the water, we piled once more into the car and headed off, this time to Guadalajara, where we still had many friends. To get there we had to cross the Sierra Madre Occidental range, which averages 7,380 feet in elevation. That figure may be unimpressive sitting on a page, but crossing it took real nerve. I still wonder how Wanda

"I Don't Know What Else It Could Have Been!"

managed to maintain a cool enough head to keep us on the road. We passed numerous little white wooden crosses standing along the roadside as we went by, some with plastic flowers bunched around them. Each cross marked the spot where someone had died in an accident. Daddy said that on winding two-lane mountain roads the bus drivers would sometimes touch the cross they kept hanging from the rearview mirror for good luck, then pull into the other lane to pass on a blind curve. That explained the places where there would be a forest of white crosses: there had been one or more bus wrecks with many fatalities.

The time came when, traveling through the mountains on a winding narrow road with steep cliffs on either side, Daddy said quietly, "Wanda, don't look down, but the gas gauge is on empty."

"Daddy, what should I do? There's no room to turn around and go back!"

"It wouldn't matter if there were. It's been hours since the last gas station."

"What can I do, Daddy?" Wanda was fighting to keep the panic out of her voice. "If we stop and can't get going, the trucks and buses are going to slam into us and—"

"You keep on driving. That's your job. I'll be praying. That's my job."

The car was quiet, the tension palpable. All of us prayed. Millie whimpered quietly, curled up against Mama and burying her face against her shoulder. Mama softly sang the song "Under His Wings": "Under His wings I am safely abiding; though the night deepens and tempests are wild, still I can trust Him; I know He will keep me; He has redeemed me, and I am His child."[1] As we twisted through the mountains, the words of the song comforted me and kept panic at bay.

Thirty miles later we suddenly came upon a narrow turnoff, and Wanda pulled over. The car quit, out of gas. Wanda's shoulders slumped in exhaustion and relief.

"Thank You, Lord! You've been with us this whole way, and You're with us now," Daddy prayed aloud. "And now, God, You know we must have gas. Please fill that need!"

Suddenly a white pickup truck pulled up behind us. A tall, handsome man—young-looking but with white hair—dressed in white shirt and pants and carrying a white gas can, got out and walked over to the driver's side window. "Are you folks out of gas?" he asked. "I think I can help you out with that." He poured the contents of the gas can into our tank. When we looked back, he and the truck had vanished.

"Mom, was that an angel?" asked Millie, awestruck.

"I don't know what else it could have been!" she answered. Before resuming our trip, we bowed our heads in joyful, reverent praise.

I remember that as if it were today. It was so awesome to have seen an angel!

Guadalajara

It was a relief to pull into the mission at Guadalajara later that afternoon. In the intervening twelve years since we had left, some of our friends had moved on, but many were still there. Sabbath School and church were a wonderful homecoming, greeting old friends with lots of *abrazos y besos* (hugs and kisses) on the cheek. They were amazed at how Wanda and I had grown, of course, and had to be told all the happenings of our lives. I didn't remember all the people, since I was so little when we left, but I did remember some of them.

Our longtime friends, the Wonchees, invited us over for dinner. Mrs. Wonchee had prepared a sumptuous seven-course meal, brought in course by course, from the potato soup through the main dish and so on until dessert. I was feeling too crammed with food to keep going, but Mama whispered, "Eat it all! In Mexico, it's rude to leave food on your plate!" So I kept eating. Afterward we walked out in their courtyard to visit. The brightly colored birds and dazzling sunshine brought back long-buried memories of the courtyard in our Mexican home.

After several days of relaxing and visiting, we were off to one last destination: Mexico City. It sits surrounded by mountains on a high plateau at an altitude of 7,300 feet. Still, the road from Guadalajara to Mexico City is not as frightening as the road to Guadalajara had been. But the roads *inside* Mexico City were another matter entirely.

Here we were, dragging our trailer behind us, in the midst of utter pandemonium. It reminded me of a swarm of just-hatched beetles completely covering the ground as they crawled about, all headed different directions and none of them getting anywhere fast. Weren't there traffic signals? Indeed there were! But it seemed that nobody so much as glanced at them. Weren't there rules about which lanes to use when turning? If there were, no one was following them. Everyone seemed to

"I Don't Know What Else It Could Have Been!"

be yelling at the top of their lungs, sitting on their horns, or driving an ambulance with the siren blaring. Why the place wasn't enmeshed in total gridlock was beyond my comprehension. Cops were everywhere, but other than waving their arms and yelling, I couldn't figure out what their function was. We obviously couldn't turn to them for help getting out of this mess.

Fortunately, we weren't in this by ourselves. Did I mention Jorge and Miguel? Jorge was the son of someone my parents knew, and Miguel was his friend. Knowing what Mexico City was like, Jorge's parents had volunteered their son to help with the driving. One look at the three young ladies in our family, and Jorge and Miguel were happy to help.

Wanda was beyond thankful not to have to drive in this mess. Amazingly, Jorge was able to negotiate Mexico City traffic. How he did it, I do not know! But he was able to get us to a trailer park, where we turned in for the night and fell into a grateful slumber.

Those two young men not only drove for us but also served as guides on a tour of some of Mexico City's most beautiful treasures. As they took us from place to place, Wanda and I began to realize that we were being pursued! Both of them were sweet and polite to our entire family, but Jorge was especially nice to me. And Wanda noticed that Miguel was being extra attentive to her.

That being the case, no one was surprised when the two young men asked Daddy for permission to date Wanda and me. Daddy smilingly told them that Wanda had a boyfriend back in the States and that at age fifteen, I was far too young to date Jorge, who was in his twenties.

Lake Xochimilco was a highlight I will never forget. We rented a large, brightly painted boat that came complete with a mariachi band (for the uninitiated, a mariachi band is a group of musicians, usually all male, in fancy matching outfits, playing trumpets and stringed instruments and singing Mexican music). I noticed Mama listening eagerly, becoming wistfully nostalgic. In the entire twelve years since we had moved to the States, Mama had never once complained about leaving her country, but watching her, I could tell how much this trip meant to her.

It had been three weeks since we had set out from home, and now it was time to be heading back. We girls had a new year of school ahead of us, and Mama and Daddy were well enough that they would soon be going back to work.

Beyond Ashes

The month we spent on that vacation was just what the family needed, after all our horror, to rejoin the rest of the world and once more begin living life to the fullest.

---

1. W. O. Cushing, "Under His Wings," *The Seventh-day Adventist Hymnal* (Washington, DC: Review and Herald®, 1985), no. 529.

CHAPTER 12

We Were So Lucky!

Back home again, it was almost time for school to start. On the Sunday before the beginning of school, we drove out to get Millie and me registered. My friends and I were hanging out on the front porch, talking about our new teacher. They said he was young and good-looking and had wavy black hair.

Then a car drove up and parked in front of the school. The driver's side car door opened, and a robust young man leaned out and opened the back door, grabbed a wheelchair with one hand, pulled it around to his door, opened it, and plopped onto it.

I just stood there, flabbergasted! The giggles around me told me that I was the last one in on the news that our new teacher was a double amputee. My friends had conspired to keep it from me so it would be a surprise.

I walked to meet him, thinking I could help. He had a big smile on his face as he quickly rolled the chair toward me. I smiled at him and he said, "You must be Marlyn. I am your new teacher. I must tell you, you have a million-dollar smile." I immediately felt endeared to him!

That was the beginning of an extraordinary school year.

Most people, if they are lucky, have one teacher during their lifetime who is funny and wise and caring and smart, who somehow makes each student in the class feel that he or she is the one the teacher cares about most. Mr. Funkhouser was that teacher, not only for me but for just about every student in the class. I like to think he really did have a soft spot in his heart for me in particular, though, because he knew about my family's tragedy, and he, too, had been through the fire of suffering.

"If only I'd stayed awake"
[The following section is my recollection of the story Mr. Funkhouser told us

Beyond Ashes

about the accident that changed his life, with adaptations and quotes from the book Funky, *by Barbara Herrera]*[1]

Lloyd Funkhouser had been attending Pacific Union College, where he was enrolled in the ministerial program and was also well-known on campus as an athlete. He had rented a small cottage near campus where he lived with his ailing mother after his stepdad had died from cancer. He did his best to care for her. But he was taking a full class load while working full time on the evening shift as an orderly at Napa State Hospital, a psychiatric facility some thirty miles distant. It might have been almost doable had he owned a car, but he did not; so he had to hitchhike there and back each day. After getting off work at eleven o'clock at night with seven-and-a-half hours to divide between sleep and study, sometimes he arrived back on campus the next day just as his classes were over at noon.

Crazy with exhaustion, falling further and further behind with his class assignments, and watching his mother weakening as the days passed, he went from depression into despair. One day he yelled aloud at God, "I said I'd serve You, and that's what I meant to do. I've put everything I've got into it." Lloyd felt as though God had let him down. "I'm going to have to give up everything unless You step in and do something. It doesn't make sense to go on like this. Nothing makes sense anymore. Please do something, Lord. I can't! Either do something, or I'll quit."

The next morning, thinking about his ultimatum to God, Lloyd felt a foreboding. It occurred to him that he had dared God—either do something, or else!—and the idea frightened him. Who was he to tell God what to do? What might be God's answer to his belligerent demand? That afternoon Lloyd gratefully accepted the offer of a ride from his friend Tom to the hospital.

Heading back to college late that night, heavy fog blanketed the road. Lloyd stuck his head out the window to watch the side of the road. He could have helped Tom steer the truck, but his eyelids felt heavy and his head drooped as he dozed off. Suddenly he was jerked awake by a scream. It was Tom, screaming as his truck careened off the road into a shallow creek.

Mr. Funkhouser told us how he went flying through the air, and everything went black. Moments later he came to, lying in the muddy creek bed underneath the truck. Under his head he could feel something slick and thick—toes. *Must be Tom's toes,* he thought, *and I must be lying here*

We Were So Lucky!

on top of him. But then Tom appeared above him, frantically calling his name. And Mr. Funkhouser realized those were his own toes. He was doubled in two and his back must be broken! *So this is it. This is what it's like to die.* "Dazed, Lloyd began to feel an almost detached sense of wonder. Probably he was dying. But he felt so much at peace. He sensed what seemed like a comforting presence—an angel, he thought—so real that he knew he could touch it if he could only reach out his arm. He could touch an angel. The idea filled him with wonder, and he felt the desire to make his own peace."

Mr. Funkhouser told us that while Tom went for help, he talked to God. He told God he didn't want to die. "God," he said, "I've been stumbling through life in a groggy daze. I haven't eaten right, and hardly slept in weeks. I let myself get worked up out of proportion to the problem. That's why I went to sleep. If only I'd stayed awake I could've helped Tom steer the truck through the fog and not gone off the cliff. I've brought this upon myself. I may die, but I'm still alive and You must love me—whatever happens, I trust You." When the ambulance finally arrived, the doctor declared it a miracle that Lloyd was alive and talking.

Transcendent joy

As Mr. Funkhouser told us the story, I came to believe that it was the decision he made that night to choose to trust God that resulted in the transcendent joy that came to define his life.

Years of hospitalization and multiple surgeries followed. Both legs had to be amputated, and then, bit by bit, shards of bone were removed from his buttocks. But the time came when he was able to go back to Pacific Union College and finish his degree—in education instead of theology. And now, ten years post-accident, he was our teacher. We were so lucky!

There were a dozen of us ninth and tenth graders in the classroom that year. He ably taught us math, science, and all our other subjects. But the most important thing he taught us was something for which no grade would ever be assigned: that he loved us and God loved us, and that with God the most terrible tragedy could end in happiness.

How can I describe this man's joy? It twinkled from his eyes, radiated from his face, rolled out in laughter as he told us funny stories and played practical jokes on us. It was the message my ragged, grieving heart needed: that no matter how deep one's suffering, God can carry that person in His arms to a place of bubbling joy. If Mr. Funkhouser had simply told me this truth, I would not have believed it; but the testimony of his life could not be denied.

Silly jokes, sports, and choir
OK, here's one for you: "One day I was sitting on the front porch of the Saint Helena Hospital where I was being treated. To pass the time, I was bouncing a rubber ball. But of course, it eventually got away from me and went bouncing over in the direction of a snobby little old lady sitting beside me on the porch. I nicely asked her to give it back, but she refused. Well, I noticed that she had a brown bag sitting next to her chair, so I leaned over and grabbed the bag. She became very angry and demanded it back. I told her I'd be happy to do that as soon as she gave me my ball back, but she still refused.

"She told me she'd report me to the director of the hospital if I didn't give it back, but I was always in trouble with him anyway for playing practical jokes on the nurses, so I didn't care."

"Did you look in the bag?" we all wanted to know.

"Yes, I did. And by now she was very agitated."

"Well, what was in it?"

"Oh, I couldn't tell you that. It would be way too embarrassing. Well, that's the end of the story." He opened his science textbook and leafed through it as if ready to teach the next class.

By now we were crazy with curiosity. "What was in it? Come on, Mr. Funkhouser! What was in it?"

He was in his element now, tantalizing us by pretending not to want to tell us as we pleaded with him. Finally he relented. "It was full of baloney, just like the rest of the story!" There was an instant of silence as we absorbed that, then laughter as it sank in how completely he had duped us.

Before his accident, he had been a well-known athlete, playing basketball and baseball and engaging in competitive swimming. Now wheelchair-bound, he still found ways to participate in sports. He pitched for our baseball teams and played volleyball from his wheelchair—and was better than just about any of us students!

High on Mr. Funkhouser's list of things he wanted to accomplish that year was to make us into a choir. Our dozen ninth- and tenth-grade students, combined with the twenty-five seventh and eighth graders, comprised the choir: every single one of us, those who could carry a tune as well as those who could not. Somehow he taught us all how to sing on tune and eventually coaxed a rich, beautiful texture out of us. Then he took us from one church to another, giving concerts. We traveled as far as Reno, Nevada, where we gave a church concert and sang the "Hallelujah Chorus" on the local TV station.

His wife, Ila Mae, had been his nurse during his hospitalization, and he had courted her from his bed. Sometimes the two of them would have us over for fun and games on a Saturday night. One evening, he and Ila Mae taught us the correct way to address the King of Siam. We were supposed to say, *"Owah—tagu—Siam."* Together we chanted this over and over, faster and faster, until one by one we realized we were saying, "Oh what a goose I am!" By then we were all collapsed on the floor laughing.

Class trip to Yosemite
Four tenth graders—Darlene, Jimmy, Judy, and I—would be going away to boarding school the following year, and Mr. Funkhouser, along with the parents of one of the four, wanted to treat us to a class trip to Yosemite. We discussed fund-raising ideas. Mr. Funkhouser puckishly suggested standing at the gym door after a Saturday night social, holding collection plates and saying, "Give to the cause!" Then if people asked what the cause was, we would say, "Cause we need it!" What we actually did, though, was to show nature movies in the school gymnasium, selling tickets to the events and selling popcorn, punch, and homemade cookies to the people who came. We raised additional money by conducting car washes. Our fund-raising efforts fell short, so the Funkhousers, along with our sponsors, chipped in the rest.

Finally the school year was over and we were on our way! We girls were in the station wagon driven by the Funkhousers. In those days before seat belts and car air-conditioning, the best way to get cool was to lie in the back, stick your legs out the back window, and wave at the trucks as they passed, honking their hellos at us.

Yosemite—wow! I had had no idea! Massive stone monoliths flanked the valley floor: quiet meadows, sparkling diamond-studded lakes, waterfalls tumbling gracefully to earth. We giggly teenagers found ourselves subdued, awed by the lavish beauty and solemn splendor surrounding us.

Beyond Ashes

We camped by a pure, clear stream. Swimming and sunbathing, cooking our food over a campfire, attending evening presentations by the park rangers, watching the firefall just after dusk each night, watching the bears raiding the garbage at night—we were having the time of our lives! On Sabbath we held Sabbath School and church service in the small amphitheater, with Mr. Funkhouser giving the sermon in his own inimitable way.

The one thing that stands out in my mind, though, is our climb up Glacier Point. It is four miles of seemingly perpendicular trail, exhausting but exhilarating. Our classmate Judy showed herself to be a little mountain goat, while Darlene and I struggled slowly upward behind her. The higher we climbed, the more spectacular the views: El Capitan, Yosemite Falls, and Half Dome. At the top we were rewarded with a snack shop where we bought ice cream; almost equally important, we found restrooms there! Believe it or not, there's a road that goes right up to the top, coming from behind, and Mr. Funkhouser had driven up to meet us.

The four days there went by all too fast, and then we were headed home. Before long, I would be leaving home to attend Lodi Academy, where Darlene and I would room together. Was I ready to leave home for boarding school? I wasn't sure.

---

1. Barbara Herrera, *Funky* (Mountain View, CA: Pacific Press®, 1978), 3–17.

CHAPTER 13

Look Out, Lodi—Here I Come!

Eucalyptus in two stately columns lined the driveway to Lodi Academy, the place that would be my home for the next two years. For the first time in my life, I would be living away from home.

Mama and Daddy helped carry my things into the girls' dorm, where we met the girls' dean, Irene Hamilton. The erectness of her posture told me that she was not a laid-back person, but the twinkle in her eyes said she loved her life and the people in it. She showed us to my room on the bottom floor, telling us on the way about the remodeling the rooms had received during the summer. Darlene, my roommate for the year, was already there and was hanging her clothes in one side of the closet. At a boarding school, having the right roommate can make a huge difference, and Darlene and I were kindred spirits!

That evening the entire student body met for orientation. Principal Will welcomed us to the campus. The theme of his talk was the idea that each of us is an individual. The things we think about today, and the choices we make today, will be who we are tomorrow. He encouraged us to become thinkers and not merely reflectors of others' thoughts, but to make good choices. Next, Principal Will explained a bounty of rules in a way that made them seem practical and like good ideas. When he introduced the faculty, I was impressed with the number of electives they offered—subjects such as home economics, printing, first aid, auto mechanics, and home nursing.

The very next day, classes started! Lights came on in all the rooms at six o'clock, with worship in the girls' dorm at six forty-five. Then breakfast in the cafeteria at seven-fifteen, followed by first-period class at eight o'clock. I could tell right away that English and history were going to be fun but that science would be pretty hard.

Beyond Ashes

After classes were finished for the day at one thirty, it was time for work. Everyone was expected to have a job, even if their parents could afford to pay their entire bill—which most parents definitely could not! My job assignment was in the cafeteria, where I was given the responsibility of making all the salads and putting them into serving-size bowls, and then working on the cleanup crew after each meal. I put in as many hours as the school allowed, making the tuition load as easy as possible on my parents.

After supper came evening worship, then study hall. We were all supposed to stay in our rooms studying from seven o'clock until nine-thirty, with no noise tolerated. Sometimes Darlene and I got into giggle-fests, but for the most part we studied hard, and I made the honor roll both my junior and senior years. At ten o'clock it was lights out in all the rooms, and the dean made the rounds to make sure everyone was present and accounted for.

So we settled into the steady routine, the rhythms of boarding academy. The rules were many—no public displays of affection, absolutely no cutting classes—but they couldn't keep us from having fun. At Girls' Open House, for instance, there was a competition to see whose room could be most creatively decorated. Darlene and I decorated our room with potted plants, borrowed from our moms, and situated our beds catty-corner. And guess what! We won first prize!

At Lodi there were no proms; we had banquets instead. The gym would be decorated in exotic themes, and we girls dressed up in chiffon and satin, and the guys in suits. That February was our first banquet. Our moms had bought us beautiful dresses: Darlene's dress was lavender, mine was pink. On the night of the banquet, we girls huddled together nervously, waiting for our dates to call us to the lobby. Then it came over the loudspeaker: "Marlyn Olsen, please come to the lobby. Darlene Wyrick, please come to the lobby." Bob and Jim were there waiting for us and struggled clumsily to pin our corsages to our dresses. We giggled as we stood there, refusing to help them. We had a wonderful time! The theme was "Some Enchanted Evening," and the food and entertainment were great.

Twice a year the school had a special week of spiritual emphasis designed to bring us closer to God. Often during those weeks, even the toughest guys walked to the front of the auditorium to receive Jesus

Look Out, Lodi—Here I Come!

Christ as their Savior. Rooms were made available for counseling and prayer. It was a good place for me to be, and the pastor's talks inspired me to take serious account of my life and to begin each morning with a scripture devotional and prayer.

The rules at Lodi were strict. I realize some people hate rules like that. I've never understood their attitude. We regarded the rules there as a source of free entertainment, a challenge to be met and mastered.

During study hall, for instance, we were supposed to be in our own rooms studying. But if Mrs. Hamilton was gone for an evening, we and some of our friends would quietly leave our rooms, wearing socks in lieu of roller skates. We'd go running full tilt down the hall, then halfway down go into a slide for the rest of the way to the other end. We didn't dare keep this up too long. Who knew when she might be back? We didn't really worry, however, because we knew Mrs. Hamilton had a ready wit and appreciated good clean fun. Her laid-out rule was: you can have fun as long as you don't do anything to hurt yourself, hurt anyone else, or break anything. She had reared a family of her own and knew teenage girls are quick to think up ideas. It seemed she was always one jump ahead of us. It was amusing, like playing cat-and-mouse.

One time, when we were disgruntled about getting in trouble for something—I've forgotten what it was—we came up with the whimsical idea to make a "tonic" out of a concoction of stuff: the remains of a cigarette butt dropped on the sidewalk by a visitor, some Lysol concentrate, fermented apple juice we had left in a closet and forgotten about, and essence of moldy cheese I found in the kitchen at work. Yuck—it stank something awful! To improve the odor—it didn't—we stirred in strong perfume. We put it in a fancy bottle, which we decorated with a piece of blue ribbon, and wrapped it up to give to our dean. We spent a while daring each other to give it to her and eventually gave up the idea because we were both too chicken. It became our private joke, and we'd recall it sometimes when we were down and needed a laugh.

Come to think of it, maybe the thing we had been in trouble for was smearing the toilet seats in our dorm with peanut butter and honey. We spread it thin enough that you would never see it if you were in any kind of hurry, so several girls sat in it before it got washed off. How did we get caught? I don't know. We thought the bathroom was empty when we did it!

Beyond Ashes

One bit of drama involving a guy took place that first year. It happened like this: The summer before academy I had met Matt at a church picnic and he asked me out on a date. I was sixteen at the time. I asked Daddy's permission, and he actually said yes! But then Frank burst into the room. "You can't let her go, Dad! Everyone knows about Matt! He's wild, and everybody knows what happens when he gets a girl in a car!" Well, that changed things, and Daddy said, *"No!"* Oh well, no big deal.

But at Lodi that year, I received a letter from Matt, and we began writing back and forth. Obviously, I didn't tell Daddy. It was about the middle of first semester that he wrote to tell me that he and his parents would be driving past Lodi to visit his sister who lived in Stockton. Could I go? He said not to worry, his parents were as strict as my dad and it would be OK.

I called Daddy and he said, *"No!"* Of course, I talked with some of my friends, and they all agreed that Daddy was too strict. I should check myself out like I was going home (it was home leave weekend) and go anyway. After all, I *was* sixteen. So that's what I did.

I checked myself out and joined Matt's family in the car, and we drove to his sister's house. After a pleasant evening of conversation, we turned in, with me on the living room couch. I fell asleep feeling smug about my little adventure, which actually was turning out to be exceedingly tame.

Early the next morning, I was awakened by men's voices. "I'm so sorry, Mr. Olsen—I was given to believe she had your permission."

"I'm sorry, too. It's not your fault, but she's coming with us—now!"

I groaned. How did Daddy figure out where I was? Now I heard Frank's voice entering the mix of conversation. I might have known. I reached for my clothing and headed for the bathroom to change.

"Thought you'd get away with it, didn't you? Dad called you, and the dean said you were gone. It took a little detective work, but we found you, all right!" All the way back to Lodi, Frank sat in the front seat of the car next to Daddy and teased me. I sat in silence, simultaneously sheepish and furious. Finally we were back at Lodi, where I was dropped off. I knew that next would be a talk with Mr. Will, the principal. What would my punishment be? To my huge relief, Mr. Will decided that it was a parental issue and left me to the tender mercies of my father.

The postscript to this occurred the summer after I turned eighteen, when I ran into Matt again, and he asked me out. He was twenty and

Look Out, Lodi—Here I Come!

handsome, and now he had his own car. Daddy said that I was eighteen and would have to make my own decision, but he set a curfew for eleven o'clock and required that it be a double date. Matt drove us to a drive-in movie in Sacramento, and we watched a John Wayne western—so far, so good.

It was on the way home that the trouble started. Matt decided to take a back road, one that was narrow and tortuous. He drove so fast that time after time he nearly lost control of the car, and over half the time he drove us on the wrong side of the road. I was scared to death—the cliff was on my side of the road! I kept pleading with him to slow down, but it just made him drive faster. It was one o'clock in the morning when he got me home to Weimar. Daddy was waiting up and stormed out to the car, where he had words for Matt like only a father can.

Afterward I told Daddy not to worry; I would never want to go out with Matt again. He was an insane driver. So Frank had the last laugh on that one!

Soon after the beginning of our senior year, the ninety of us in our graduating class got together in a large classroom to choose class officers. I was kind of zoned out, not following proceedings very closely, when I heard my name mentioned and realized they were nominating me to be vice president of our senior class. What? Me being nominated? I didn't consider myself part of the "in" group, and the others nominated were definitely part of the campus elite. It blew me away when they announced that I was the winner of the vote, but I felt honored. What an adventure to be a class officer and to be in on planning the senior snow trip to Wawona as well as other events, and ultimately graduation.

I had a new job that year, grading history papers in the boys' dormitory for Mr. Leslie Bietz, who was my history teacher and the boys' dean. I worked in his office, which had an open doorway and was located in the front. Boys would stop by to chat and would try to get me to tell them what would be on the tests. "Who is buried in Grant's tomb?" "What state is Lodi in?" Ha, did they ever learn when I gave them ridiculous questions! While working in the dorm, I had a few friends who were boys—like brothers, and that's how I liked it.

Darlene was not able to return her senior year, so I roomed with Pam and Lennie in the dorm's one oversize room. Pam was outgoing, bubbly, and full of fun. She often provided special music in her beautiful

Beyond Ashes

contralto voice, sometimes singing solos, and other times in a ladies' trio.

One evening we heard that our dean, Mrs. Hamilton, was away for the evening—where, we didn't know. All we knew was that she was gone, which meant we were on our own! The girls' dorm had a courtyard shaped like so: Π, with a high fence at the open end and just beyond it, the administration building. In the absence of clothes dryers, the school had put up clotheslines in the courtyard where we girls could hang our laundry. Pam, Lennie, and I had just finished washing our clothes and had gone out to the clothesline to pin them up. After all, the dean was off to parts unknown, and how was she going to know we weren't in our rooms studying like we were supposed to be? No one would ever rat us out—that much we knew for sure!

As we worked, Pam started singing a silly ditty about our dean to the tune of "Goodnight Irene," a song we often sang to her. Today, however, she made up new words as she went along. Something like this:

Goodnight, Irene goodnight,
We won't see you in our dreams,
Cuz we ain't babies, we are teens
We'll see you in our nightmares.
Goodnight Irene, Irene goodnight, goodnight Irene,
Irene goodnight, goodnight Irene, we'll see you in . . .

Lennie and I joined in, the three of us singing at the top of our lungs and giggling between verses. Suddenly I realized a familiar voice was calling my name—all our names! "Marlyn, Pam, Lennie! Stop your racket and come with me!" It was Miss Lund, our principal's secretary. She had been trying to get our attention for several minutes, and we had been singing so loudly that she hadn't been able to make herself heard. We stopped singing. Dead silence.

"Girls, please come with me."

We followed single file, barefooted and crimson-faced. The next minute we were in the administration building, in the room nearest the fence and the clotheslines. Ten people in business attire were seated around a table, among them our dean. It was the monthly school board meeting, and they had heard our entire performance! All present wore solemn expressions, which they were doing their best to maintain.

Look Out, Lodi—Here I Come!

I will spare you the ignominy of the minutes that followed. I will just say that we were sentenced to a day of hard labor washing down the walls of the main hallway in the girls' dorm, and our class absences were all counted as unexcused. We finished the job in one day, because we knew that if it took us longer, we would have to just keep at it for as many days as it took.

And as we worked, we sang every silly ditty we could think of.

"Shinier than I've ever seen these walls before," remarked Mrs. Hamilton with a hint of humor in her voice.

Little by little, I was developing a reputation as the unofficial counseling therapist of the girls' dorm. I had walked through the fire of loss and grief, and it gave me an instant empathy with girls who had family problems, boyfriend problems, and teacher problems, or whatever else. I was short on wise advice—offered some when asked—but long on listening and sympathy. I began to see how important listening was.

Near the end of the year was the senior class trip. What a blast! We rode the academy bus to Wawona, a tourist town located within Yosemite National Park. The natural beauty of the place is legendary, with so many things to see. At an elevation of four thousand feet, the place was still snowy in late spring, so we went skiing. I was queen of the bunny slope, and even though I wasn't exactly a great skier, I had fun!

All too soon, graduation day came. Dressed in white gowns, blue tassels tickling our noses, the ninety of us lined up outside the auditorium awaiting our grand entrance. What an honor to march next to the president of the class as the vice president to begin the processional. I strained to see Mama, Daddy, Wanda, and Millie in the crowded auditorium. There they were, looking proud. Then came the walk across the stage for the handshake and the diploma and the words, "Marlyn Olsen, graduating with honors." A quick pose for picture-takers, then a big smile as I spotted my family, beaming, waving, blowing kisses, and clapping hard for me! Then came the ritual of throwing graduation hats into the air, the tearful hugs and kisses with classmates we might never see again, and finally packing and moving out of the dorm.

Graduation brought the story of 1960–1961 to a close. It meant parting from close friends and returning to home life for the summer. Now Lodi was just a memory, one I would cherish forever.

With Mama's help I landed a full-time summer job at Weimar

Beyond Ashes

Sanitarium working as a nursing assistant. Looking back now, working to help pay my way through college was one of the best things that ever happened to me. Best of all, I especially enjoyed working with Mama.

Next would be college.

CHAPTER 14

Kaleidoscope of Fun and Fanfare

Whoever penned the words "all things bright and beautiful" could've been sitting on my shoulder as I gazed at the beauty of my new home. Giant palms waving in the breeze, bright-colored berries on pepper trees, and rows of flower beds on manicured lawns. I sang, danced, and laughed all at once—college at last!

In the midst of the buzz, a glitch—my planned-for roommate had decided to attend a college in her hometown. Rooming with a complete stranger could be hit-or-miss. When I entered the ladies' residence hall, Dean Lena Cady's smile put my mind at ease. I'd reached utopia—what could go wrong?

"Follow me to room 107. I'll introduce you to Marcie. You two will be a good match!"

First impressions hinted awkwardness, but Marcie was a country rustic like me. Soon we chitchatted like parrots at a gabfest.

"Wow! Nifty outfits! Mind if I borrow?" I asked.

"We look to be the same size," Marcie said as she reached for a dress in her closet. "And this dress is just your color."

"Red—my favorite! How'd you know?"

Daddy toured the grounds. Mama browsed the campus market. Soon they returned looking satisfied.

"Sandwiches, bananas, and treats to paunch our bellies. And I made a few discoveries! Nature is expansive behind the campus—three hundred acres of pastureland, and hills galore—hiking trails winding up the mountains!" Daddy gesticulated with relish as he devoured a sandwich.

Mama shuddered. "You can be sure there are rattlesnakes in those mountains and *cougars*. Promise me you will be careful. You must never *ever* hike alone!"

Beyond Ashes

"Cross my heart, Mama, *and I don't hope to die*, but you know how trouble follows me."

"Yes, the devil has tried to kill you many times. There is no doubt God has protected you over and over. Still I worry, child. What in the world is going to happen to you next?"

"Marlyn, you and I are cut out of the same cloth. Surely angels work overtime. Try not to wear yours out." Daddy winked at me while placing a hand on Mama's shoulder. "Your mom and I don't want to spoil your fun, but please do exercise caution."

Mama motioned for me to sit on her lap. I snuggled in as she sang "A La Rue Rue Niña."

If I were a puppy, I would've wagged my tail.

"I'll miss you, *Boquita Linda* [Mama's term of endearment for me]. Promise me you'll write once a week. I want to know everything, even your adventures."

"Come join our prayer circle." Daddy offered a hand to Marcie as our family gathered around. "Thank You, Father, that angels who are continually beholding Your face are watching over Marlyn and Marcie. I leave them in Your care. And I ask for an umbrella of protection over Mother and me on our trip home."

I watched as my family climbed into the car and Daddy gripped the steering wheel with worn-out Nappa gloves. Soon the car disappeared out of sight. Mama and Daddy would spend the night with friends in Loma Linda, then head for home in the morning. My new friend and I raced to the room, ready to tackle new adventures.

"Your parents are out-of-sight cool! How lucky! My parents abandoned me when I was four," Marcie's voice faltered. "Last I remember them, they dropped me off at Grandma's and took off to who-knows-where. Now Grandma is getting on in age, and I'm here to snatch a husband. Wish me luck!" Marcie's openness and generous spirit drew me in. We became exceptionally good friends.

Orientation began with luncheon on the cafeteria lawn. Dean of students, George Akers, stood to speak. "I pledge assistance in every way I can. It's my plan to become individually acquainted with each of you. There's a sign-up sheet in the lobby of the ad building. You may circle an appointment time to fit your schedule. The door of my office is always open." I was impressed with his friendliness.

Kaleidoscope of Fun and Fanfare

Dean Akers proceeded by detailing a few facts about the campus community: "1,080 students from thirty-eight states and twenty-four foreign countries, two women's dormitories, two men's dormitories, village students and commuters from nearby towns, classes a short walk from the dorm, campus community shops providing needed living essentials, rest and relaxation aplenty, weekly social events, swimming pools, fitness rooms, horseback riding, waterskiing, hiking, camping in the mountains, and ..." There was a major roar—hand clapping and whistles rolled a chuckle in the dean's chest. "Now the bottom line of why you are here—you'll be divided into small groups, appointed an upper-class student leader, and given a guided tour of the campus and classrooms. Thereafter you will meet in the homes of faculty members and be given the opportunity to ask questions."

Orientation proved fascinating. Relationships with the dean and faculty were well-defined, characterized by amiable cooperation. Marcie and I felt radiant and confident. Tomorrow we would meet with academic advisors who would assist in choosing a course of study. I had registered as a nursing major, but following the career assessment test, I took a one-eighty switch to an education major. Classes began Monday morning.

The world of academia

Professor of English and literature Merlin Neff, book editor for Pacific Press Publishing Association and author of numerous books, had accepted the call that year to assume responsibilities as head of the departments of English and Journalism, as well as to chair the Division of Languages and Literature. New to the campus, his objective was to foster creative writing skills, which he felt were needed in the line of Christian books and publications. As part of the process, he inaugurated the idea of an English placement test that included compositional writing. Students scoring the highest were placed in his class. I was pleased to qualify in the top thirty. Professor Neff's earnest and supportive style of teaching inspired the students to do their best. At the end of the year he encouraged his students to pursue further writing. Thus was planted a seed that would grow. Family and friends gave thumbs up, and I assumed the role of family scribe—interviewing and taking notes. The consensus was that someday I'd write a book.

Professor of education Andrew Nelson's definition of success as a teacher was that all students must achieve an A or a B; anything lower was unacceptable, and work would have to be done over until this grade was attained.

"True education is the harmonious development of all faculties—mental, physical, spiritual, social, and emotional. Balance in each is the key word." Ouch—that hit the bull's-eye! At times my emotions felt like a roller coaster. Hmm, balance—intriguing. OK, head knowledge for an A, but …

Professor Nelson must've read my face. "God loves each one of us passionately. We are on learning grounds, and He allows slipups. Mistakes are learning stations. We don't look at them as 'should haves.' We look at them as opportunities to learn and to grow. Jesus always offers a helping hand. He helps us live a balanced life." I was pleased as punch to be in this class. The principles I learned, especially the gravity of a spiritual connection in living a balanced life, are still with me today.

Professor of religion (Life and Teachings of Jesus) Fritz Guy's method of teaching presented an uplifting vision of true Christianity as taught by Jesus and recorded in the Gospels. "True spirituality is not religion, not a set of rules. True religion is Christlikeness. Ultimately: Christianity means being so filled with Christ's love that when others look at us, they see His love shining through; Jesus came to reveal the Father's love; He is an ever-present live-in Father (in our hearts), never more than a breath away. If you walk out of this class experiencing His love and sharing it with others, I will have been successful as a teacher. It's as simple as that." Not an easy principle to follow, but I gave it my best shot.

During roll call one day, Dr. Guy asked whether I was related to M. E. Olsen, missionary to Mexico.

"He's my father."

"Your dad was a pioneer in the work of bringing the gospel to Mexico, certainly a remarkable man. So you are an MK? [Children of missionary parents are often categorized with the term MK—missionary kid.] I have a high regard for MKs." Several hands shot up when he asked if there were more. We formed ourselves into a support team. And so I became acquainted with Cindy, also an education major and in several of my classes. Unbeknownst to us then, ten years later we would meet again in the foyer of a church in Georgia the same day her father would commence as the new pastor—a zippy surprise for two California transplants new to the South. Mom Green took me under wings of care, bringing me into the family circle at church.

Professor of education and psychology George T. Simpson, in an effort to promote mind, character, and personality development, used practical means of teaching psychology. In confronting the effects of fear, students were assigned to share a childhood experience in one of three ways: in class, on paper, or privately. I chose privately. And for the first time since the night of terror, I reached into the hidden recesses of my mind and stammered out the fiery furnace experience, the loss of my brother, and the aftershocks.

"I see a composed exterior, but deep inside lurks a frightened little girl who takes care of people but does not know how to care for the wounded spirit inside."

Thereafter began the process of my learning how to break the cycle of post-fire events that at times bordered on panic attacks. Along these lines, I began learning how to address the phobias that had developed as a result of the horrific trauma: fear of the dark (running in the dark), fear of loud sounds (gas hot-water heater explosion sounding like a bomb), thanatophobia (incessant fear of death or losing loved ones), and survivor's guilt (Why Milton? Why not me?). Contemplating these ideas, a seed burst inside my brain: Should I enter the field of counseling? Dr. Simpson offered high-fives of encouragement. First, there were a few things to absorb: God's grace always provides bounce-ability in pothole experiences. I must learn to fill my own love cup before I can help others. Only in a childlike state of being born again can I receive God's unconditional love and offer it to others. When bad things happen, I have three choices: let the experience define me, let it destroy me, or let it strengthen me. Ultimately, with God *all* things are possible.

"I see in you a strong young woman who has survived this long with all the mess intact. It can't be straightened up at once. It will be a day-by-day process. Healing will take time. God allows space to learn at your own pace." As I look back, I cherish the counseling I received with Dr. Simpson. Though it took time for his message to sink in, it started my road to recovery—to look for ways God showed His love and care in the midst of all the pain and suffering I had endured.

Many more professors are forever engrained in my memory bank. I arrived thirsty for knowledge and received it in abundance.

Beyond Ashes

There was also an environmental mentor, Two-bit Hill, a knoll with a big rock overlooking hills and valleys—a private chapel in which to contemplate life and axioms, to throw open the windows of my soul.

An honorable mention goes to the girls' dean. Ms. Cady had a tough but sugarcoated discipline that made all of us want to do what was right. Her motto was, "Harsh words and acts do not benefit anyone." She dealt with the students as mature adults. Her heart held not a trace of selfishness. Each month she prepared a special meal, topped with homemade cake, for girls celebrating birthdays. A person has not really enjoyed food until he or she has tasted Ms. Cady's mouthwatering dishes. What fun it was for me to celebrate my birthday with birth-month twins when March birthdays rolled around.

Boarding college provided a loving, safe (at times crazy) home, like being part of a large, sometimes dysfunctional, family. Friends were always nearby—a wonderful mix of different personalities. I owe so much to that school and wouldn't be the person I am today without it, never again to experience the closeness, the familiarity, the love, and the friendship that happened there. I can't help feeling a little nostalgic for the boarding academy and college days that would continue into the next year.

In the next chapter, I'll tell you about the social side of my college experience—the most important!

CHAPTER 15

Finding True Love or Something Like That

The desire for love is in the DNA of the human soul. In that era, books on dating were not available. We learned by trial and error. Some girls majored in "husband hunting." Not me. I was in the spring of life, too young and not ready to give my heart. In addition, I was becoming more and more aware of the need to find myself before love found me.

Students' names became faces through the invaluable *Inside Dope*, a booklet with an ID photo of each student, designed to serve as a key to open new friendships. That's how I met Michael. As I entered the relationship, I knew I was not ready for permanency, but why not date?

Mike was an exploring, probing spirit like me. He opened my eyes to a dazzling new world, a thousand intriguing places I hadn't yet become familiar with. He was a great catch, my friends said. He was a junior pre-med student and a gifted guru in the classroom with a GPA of 4.0! A keeper! Don't let him get away!

Mike's ambition pushed me, his pride in me a motivation to be ever improving. He was my walking dictionary and thesaurus. When I was stumped by a homework problem, he offered help. Soon it would be mission accomplished, followed by a hop into his sporty car, and off to sunny beaches on the Pacific. We sat romantically gazing at the sunset; got ringside seats on a friend's lawn at the Rose Bowl Parade on New Year's Day; watched the stars at Griffith Observatory, Southern California's gateway to the cosmos; and visited Mount Palomar Observatory. An unsophisticated country girl turned sage and swept off her feet! And I could keep my grades up. How could life be better?

When President John F. Kennedy visited our campus, I had the privilege to see him up-close because of Mike being a student body officer. An entourage of secret agents mingled with the guests as they entered, while the band played "God Bless America." I was thrilled!

Beyond Ashes

Bear Mountain Ski Resort

Mike, an expert on skis, taught me how to master the basics. A rush of excitement tingled through my spine as I prepared for the slopes. As I was halfway up on the rope tow, a skier zoomed past. Easy-breezy, it seemed, but suddenly her skis crossed and she landed in a heap just a few feet away, screaming in pain. Two paramedics arrived on the scene with emergency medical equipment. They bound her leg, secured her on a sled, and towed her down the slope. My doubt about this whole idea surged. Mike came to my rescue and helped me hobble down the slope. Disenchantment with skiing gave way to a far better adventure when he rented a horse-drawn sleigh, a delightful ride with cool evening breezes against our faces. Dining in a cozy restaurant, with a roaring fireplace in the center of the room, capped the day's events. It had been a charming day!

Dead ringer

I could hardly wait to see my old roommates. The express Greyhound bus could not get me to Lodi soon enough. Lennie was getting married. Pam and I would be bridesmaids in her wedding. I thought, *I'm a bona fide college student pursuing a career, dating an upper-class guy, full-grown beyond pranks or drama—well, almost. What will they think of the new me?*

As luck would have it, I caught the bridal bouquet. Actually, it was more like Lennie launching it to me. The idea of *being next* was scary. I passed it to Pam like a hot potato. She passed it back. I placed it into the hands of a nearby hopeful—that would be my good deed for the day. The wedding was fun, colorful, and romantic, a wonderful reunion with old friends. All too soon it was time to board the bus, this time a bus that would stop at every city along the way. Claiming a seat to myself, I managed to catch a few hours of sleep, until I was abruptly jarred awake by two stony-faced police officers towering over me.

"You meet the description of a woman wanted for armed robbery. Come with us." The taller of the two spit out the words. Roughly yanking my hands behind me, they handcuffed me, dragged me off the bus, and shoved me into the back seat of a police car. Then it was off to the police station. They sat me down in a chair and proceeded to rifle through my suitcase.

"Crime doesn't pay, lady! Where'd you stash the cash? Who's your

Finding True Love or Something Like That

accomplice?" Over and over, they asked the same questions. The interrogation seemed to last for hours.

"You're wrong! I'm not the person you're looking for!" I pled again and again.

A mugshot was stuck in front of my face. "How can you deny this?"

Horror of horrors—that criminal looked like me! *A criminal? They insist I am that woman?* Scared out of my wits, I realized I had no ID with me. Muddled thoughts swam through my brain. *How on earth am I ever going to get out of this mess?*

Finally my tired brain kicked in. "I'm a student at La Sierra College in Riverside County."

"Yeah, sure."

"Please call them! They will verify what I'm saying," I cried. "Ask them if they have a Marlyn Olsen as a student."

"All right, lady, we'll give it a try." The nicer cop sauntered off, shaking his head.

"Her story checks out," he told the other cop when he returned.

"Too bad! There for a while I thought we had the perp."

The nicer officer dropped me off at the bus depot. Pointing a finger, he charged, "Young lady, I do not want to ever see you night riding on the bus by yourself again! It's not safe! And stick to your studies, you hear!" He looked at me in a fatherly kind of way. When I stepped off the bus, Mike was a welcome sight. I fell into his arms.

"What happened? When you didn't arrive as scheduled, I checked with the registrar to see if there had been a change of plans. Surely you'd get back for the Valentine's Banquet tonight."

"The banquet?" I giggled—then cracked up. "I'm sorry, once I start I can't stop," and I proceeded to convulse with laughter. Between chortles, I spilled the bizarre adventure, setting off a round of titters all the way to campus. From dread to delight—all in a day's time! The banquet was fabulous! My bridesmaid dress looked even better with a white orchid corsage, compliments of Mike.

Life was comfortable. Then alas, a setback! Mike, a believer in Christ, had begun to explore books that promoted agnosticism, the idea that it is impossible to know whether God exists. I was aghast! How could anyone question God's existence? We argued, but in the end decided to agree to disagree on the subject of God. I reasoned, *I believe in God; I love*

Beyond Ashes

Mike. Therefore, in time he will believe again. We'll just not discuss the religion thing. But the fact that he no longer believed in God in turn opened the gate to another huge upheaval. Mike, who had been respectful of my high moral ideals, was now entertaining what he called a more intimate relationship.

"We're in love. How can that be wrong?"

"I'm not ready to give my heart, body, and soul. That's what's wrong." Our relationship turned wobbly over the issue. It seemed a game to Mike, but it wasn't for me. I had made up my mind, and I stuck to my guns. After the third breakup, it was mutually agreed to call it quits—a sorrowful time for both of us.

On the last day of school, I was all packed to return home for the summer when I received a surprise call from Mike. "I'm taking a trip to Lake Tahoe next week, and driving past Weimar. I'd like to stop by."

"Sure! I'd like you to meet my parents!"

Mike strummed Mama's banjo and sang, "Lady of Spain." Mama danced and clapped her hands. Daddy interviewed him as only a father can do. He passed Daddy's scrutiny.

"I'm on my way to Lake Tahoe. I'd like to take your daughter."

"With our blessing," they chimed together.

Lawrence Welk was playing live at Harrah's Club. We enjoyed the music for a while, and then walked beside the lake under the moonlit sky.

"Marlyn, surely you must know I'm still in love with you. When you return to college in the fall, I'd like to pick up where we left off. I've given it some thought, and I promise to honor your integrity. I will not pressure you otherwise. I'm not at the point where I can propose, but I hope to when we're both ready." I was blown away.

Alas, when I returned to campus for my sophomore year, I learned that Mike had picked up with a senior student from England. I saw them eating together at the snack bar. When he didn't call, I knew it was over. He was my first love—my first heartbreak. OK—no more guys in my life—no more dating.

A few days later, as I carried an overload of books, along came a big hunk of a guy offering to carry them for me. "But first, let's get acquainted," Silas said, as he set the books down on a bench. I looked up into incredible blue eyes. How could I be spilling out my hurtful relationship with Mike to someone I'd just met? But I did. Silas was a good listener. Before I knew it, I was telling him about the fire and the loss of my little brother. When he wiped away a tear with his shirt, I felt drawn into his soul.

"Now tell me about you."

"Not much to say. I've finished a stint in the army. Old man coaxed me into college. I agreed to try it for one year."

"What's your major?"

"Adventure—not interested in a formal education. See the tennis courts, the pool, the gym? That's where I hang out. Scholastic achievement is secondary."

"Well, you are honest."

Silas was fun, exciting, while at the same time shy. What he deemed flawed, I saw reason to like: his heartwarming stutter when he became excited about life; a floppy wisp of blond hair always out of place; a shyness when wearing glasses; the way he let my compliments bounce off like a tennis ball; a sad smile accompanied by a vacant stare when talking about sad memories; his honesty about a lack of relationship with his dad, whom he labeled a control freak; his closeness to his mother. But most of all, I was drawn to his overwhelming passion for adventure. After a hurtful breakup, it seemed to be what I needed.

Silas's persona was a touch of unpredictable wonder. Like the time he took my hand and led me to the music room, then proceeded to play every instrument—piano, guitar, saxophone, flute—by ear. At chapel the next morning, a rich baritone voice sang, "How Great Thou Art." It was Silas. Another surprise: I didn't know he could sing.

Then there was the time he grabbed my hand and made me run high-speed with him. I must've been a sight running pell-mell to keep up, my straight skirt up to my thighs and right past Mike. "I have a surprise for you," he said. "Boy, have I got a surprise." Blindfolded, I was led to his new 1962 Harley-Davidson Panhead. "Paying for it myself with my part-time job. Hop on; you're in for the ride of your life! We'll hit one hundred miles per hour." He beamed.

Did I mention the cyclone roller coaster at Long Beach?

Another surprise: Silas, known as the strong man on campus, pushed weights at two hundred. I noticed girls sighing over him, especially Sharon, a freshman student, who followed him around like a puppy. "Not interested," he said. After which he sang to me the romantic song of the

Beyond Ashes

sixties, "Only You," made famous by the Platters.

I cared for Silas. He was fun and easy to talk to. But his lack of interest in scholastics, and my own worrisome decline in grades at the end of first semester, caused me to slow down the relationship. However, we remained best friends, at times eating together in the cafeteria or chatting under a palm.

Falling in love when you're not ready can break you down like a jigsaw puzzle falling apart. You thought you were a complete picture, that you had everything figured out. In my experience, one thing was entirely certain—as with Mike, Silas and I were too young; the timing was not right.

So it was back to studying for me!

CHAPTER 16

Tossed Out and Nowhere to Go

Arriving back on campus after a summer spent at home, I found disheartening changes: the college president had retired; Ms. Cady had vacated her spot as girls' dean to marry the love of her life and the girls had dubbed the new dean of women "Miss Never-a-Smile"; and George Akers, beloved dean of students, had taken a leave of absence to continue educational studies. Three loving and beloved administrators gone! What would the place be like now?

The new dean of students was introduced. We students sat inwardly groaning as he delivered his welcoming speech: "The 'getting by' attitude on campus is dangerous and deadly. I urge all staff members and faculty to give serious thought and effort to promulgating the principles upon which our college was founded in 1922. I'll pledge my earnest effort to see that this is done."

Walking back to our dorms, I heard a few students express their indignation. "Doesn't he know the year is 1962? What will become of our campus?" How serious our new dean was about this pledge, I would soon find out.

Spring break arrived the last week in March. After an unusually rainy winter, our campus again burst into the lush and colorful verdure of spring. Two-bit Hill put forth at least a dozen different varieties of flowers. Fruit trees blossomed. Bees buzzed. Birds happily serenaded the last of the sweating, pencil-biting exam-takers. Surrounded by beauty, how could I foresee the storm looming ahead of me?

Without warning, the dam broke. Wanda called with alarming news. "Mama and Daddy have split up. Our farmhouse has been rented out with the possibility of selling it. Mama has moved into a one-room nursing apartment at Weimar Sanitarium, where she still works. Daddy has purchased a tiny one-bedroom trailer and moved it to our property, where he is living now."

Beyond Ashes

"But, Wanda, what happened? What's going on?"

"I didn't want to tell you, but since you asked—you know how grief-stricken Mama was after Milton died. Well, when you left for college and Millie left for San Pasqual Academy, it seems Mama became even more despondent. She may be near a nervous breakdown. She says the house is too sorrowful for her. It has too many memories and life has no meaning without her children."

"It wouldn't have happened if I hadn't left."

"I haven't had much time for her, either. Troy is two and a half. Lisa's just a baby. What's more, Donnie works long hours."

"What do we do now?"

"I don't know, Marlyn. Daddy is taking it hard. I'll be seeing him later today, but you know Daddy; he always pulls through, so try not to worry about it."

In a daze, I lay the phone receiver in its cradle, walked down to my room, head down, and sat quietly on my bed. I felt responsible for having left Mama when she needed me so. Slowly I began to sob. Disparate emotions churned inside. I wanted to hide somewhere, to get away from reality. But there was nowhere to go.

Spring break was just around the corner. This year I had been invited to go on a "girls only" outing to Newport Beach, about an hour and a half from the college. There were eight of us. Everyone was sitting around, laughing, talking, and teasing each other. I tried to join in the gaiety of the occasion, but my emotions were miles away from all the chatter. Still, I didn't let anyone in on what was taking place inside.

Sitting at the table, unable to eat lunch, I happened to see an advertisement—a beautiful woman in a field of flowers smoking a Salem cigarette. "Enjoy the cool menthol taste of Salem, the cigarette for women." Without giving it much thought, I counted out the change in my purse, just enough to buy a pack. Casually I walked over to a cigarette vending machine. I inserted the coins into the machine and made the selection—out dropped a pack of Salem cigarettes and matches.

Unmindful of the surprised stare of several of the girls, I walked over to the table, sat down, lit a cigarette, and proceeded to suck in, but I didn't inhale. Who would want to? The stuff was *nasty*! But, maybe this would dull the hurt and frustration I felt toward my parents. How could they be separating like this? For that matter, how could I be smoking?

Tossed Out and Nowhere to Go

Mom and Dad, as well as the church schools I had attended, had taught about the harmful effects of smoking—something I said I'd never do.

My thoughts were spinning ten different directions at once. I didn't like what I was doing, but I did it anyway. *So why did I buy those cigarettes?* I looked around for a trash can where I could toss the rest of the pack. None immediately presented itself, so I stashed it in my parka, telling myself I would throw it out as soon as I got a chance, and promptly forgot all about it. As I look back, I don't think it was about rebelliousness. Instead, it was a way to cover up anxiety. The woman in the ad looked happy and cool. I wanted to be happy and cool. Did the smoking make me happy? Would I ever smoke again? *No*—it didn't. *No*—I never smoked again.

Nevertheless, I would pay bitterly for my deed. Two weeks later, Sharon, who still had a crush on Silas, decided it was her duty to report the incident to the girls' dean. My room was searched while I was in class. "Miss Never-a-Smile" found the pack, and I was called into her office. "I will have to report this to the dean of students."

One look at his steely face and I knew I was in deep trouble. "Did you buy these cigarettes?"

I nodded. "But, but, I've never ..."

"Don't lie to me, young lady! I know there are smokers on this campus—I've smelled it and you're one of them! You bought this pack and you've been caught! I have zero tolerance for smokers! I've been waiting to catch somebody! I'm going to show you and everyone else I ... will ... not ... tolerate ... smoking! You will be a lesson to everybody! You are expelled, effective immediately! You must withdraw from all your classes!"

"I am not a smoker, sir. I did buy a pack, and I even lit up, but I threw it away after a few minutes, because it was disgusting! And I have never ever been in trouble before! Check my record and you will see it's true!"

It was obvious that none of this mattered to him. He cut me off with the same rhetoric. As he spoke, I stared at him. Before me sat a man, a Bible on his desk, blinded to the spiritual reality of God as well as to my need—stuck in a pit of rigidity. I had been grounded in the amazing grace and mercy of a God who came to save, not condemn. I sat there bewildered. My heart shattered into a million pieces. I couldn't bite back the tears, but no matter. He had an agenda—a need to establish himself as a disciplinarian. No one was going to cross him. I wasn't one of the campus smokers, but I would be the scapegoat.

Some of my teachers talked to the dean, asking him to reevaluate the punishment. "It didn't happen on campus, and it took place during spring break." But to no avail.

As I withdrew from my classes, the professors offered words of sympathy. "We're sorry this is happening to as fine a student as you." Miss Prentice, the librarian, for whom I worked, offered a shoulder to cry on. My heart was comforted—but devastated nevertheless. This event would drastically affect my future. What would lie ahead?

Through the haze, a bright shaft of light appeared. I was just six weeks away from finishing my sophomore year; three and a half months of second-semester credits went down the drain. I still owed money on my bill, which my parents, because of present circumstances, could not pay. A benevolent soul stepped forward and paid the remaining debt. We never found out who.

I had lived with heartbreaks; some worse than others, like the fire tragedy. This time I lost my dream. The dream of achieving a college education was pulled from under my feet. Distressed beyond all measure, I wept nonstop. There would be no quick resolution of my pain. Bitterness—judgment toward this man—took root in my heart, not to be resolved until years later. For now, however, it dimmed my view of God.

I was repentant. I prayed. Why didn't God do something? Life seemed unfair.

In my confused state, I saw God clothed in a human man's mannerisms—a stern, hard-nosed policeman with an inability to sympathize or try to understand. In my swirling inner darkness, this idea was not resolved for quite a while. My eyes were temporarily blinded to God's love. I was a little girl lost again, stuck in a pit of hopeless despair. Would I find my way out? The following poem penned by an anonymous writer describes how I felt; it's called "The Little Girl Inside":

> I'm not the same on the outside as I am on the inside,
> I smile, I laugh, but I don't know joy.
> Where is my joy, O my God?
> Why have you forsaken me?
> Everything was once so free. . . .

Tossed Out and Nowhere to Go

Once grass was green, and hills were pretty.
Now I seem to see them through a veil of gray.
Inside is cold and tight and sad.
I cry and ache. Most days I long for eyes to see me.
I know it's me but then I think,
They don't care—God must not care.
But too long I have known His love,
And I know this is not true.
Yet, I am unable to get above
And I am sinking slowly in the sands.
"Help," I say—inside I scream—
But on my face, I smile.
Only my eyes express—the well of pain in me.
I'm careful not to look at those
Who might strip away my mask?
But I want it to come down, at last,
Reality to grasp.
I cannot do this for myself.
Am I ready for YOU at last?
"Honesty," we cry, "transparency," and the like.
But who will brave this scary turf?
I've been brave, I've tried.
But from openness came pain,
From those who want to close my door,
Who trample my little girl inside?
So light and gay is she, but oh, so sensitive,
And too many times others have driven her in.
"Come out, little girl," I coax,
But she just sits and mopes,
No longer can I coax her out,
Are you sleeping, little girl?
Lord, send someone to love her to life, once more.

Following the exile were tearful goodbyes to teachers and friends, bittersweet memories of good times, and grieving for what I left behind: two of the best years of my life on a campus I loved. A door had been slammed in my face. Where could I go?

Beyond Ashes

Seven years earlier, after the fire, I had found myself homeless. That time, kind friends had shared their home with me. Now I was once more homeless. Neither parent could give me a home. Where *could* I go?

A door opened. Aunt Alice, who was now a widow, took me under her wing. Daddy had called, asking her to look out for me. She had sold the family home and was now living in a one-bedroom apartment in Santa Monica. At least temporarily, she could take me in. I could sleep in the living room on her sofa.

CHAPTER 17

City Jungle

Have you ever felt like you were stuck, in a slump? Like someone hit the pause button and you were smacked by a lull in the action? Focusing on the past would keep me stuck. I was where I was—*a new starting point, not my ending point*—a new adventure. The day I arrived, outside the day was calm and bright, but inside my heart was thumping. I felt bewildered, but not abandoned. I asked God for direction. I needed a job. The next morning a friend of Aunt Alice's called, saying, "There's a temporary private duty assignment in a nursing home two blocks from where you live, and it starts immediately. Would your niece be interested?"

Would I! I had several months' experience working with the elderly—"Yes!" I quickly responded, and made a beeline to the nursing home. There I was interviewed by the supervisor.

"Mrs. Breckenridge is recovering from hip replacement. Let me warn you, her ready wit and sharp mind will require special attention. They come and go with her. Follow me and I'll introduce you."

Mrs. Breckenridge leaned forward in her wheelchair, sizing me up. Elbows jutted to each side like those of a tightrope walker gripping a balance pole. "You look too skinny to be of much help. Let's see if you can assist me into the bathroom. *Humph*, you're stronger than I thought. Now help me into bed." She barked one order after the other until everything was done to her satisfaction.

"That's a mighty pretty young lady in the picture. Is that your daughter?"

"*Humph*, yeah, but she never comes to see me. She thinks I'm a caviling old woman. Really, I'm not; it's the staff—brusque is what they are! Can you blame me? And the food? Rotten to the core. You know, I like you. You're the most attentive nurse I've had in a long time. As soon as I recover, number one on my bucket list is a trip around the world on an ocean liner. How about making an old woman happy and accompanying me as my nursemaid? I would pay all your expenses. What do you say?"

"It's been my dream to travel the world."

"Settled—in the interim, you must live with me in my apartment until I'm fully recovered. I'll pay you in addition to providing free room and board. Soon we'll sail the high seas."

There is a popular saying, "If it seems too good to be true, it probably is." Oblivious to that, I relocated to her upscale apartment in Beverly Hills. Mrs. Breckenridge managed well with her cane and followed me into every nook and cranny of her apartment. Ironhanded and bossy would be a mild way to describe her. The low wages she paid were certainly earned. When I brought up the idea of travel, she changed the subject. On one of our excursions outside, I noticed an employment agency a few blocks down the street. During my lunch break I darted over and filled out an application. I listed office work in Santa Monica as my first choice for employment. As I daydreamed about a job in a fancy office, a handsome man with movie-star good looks called out my name.

"My name is Neal," he said as he extended his hand.

"Pleased to meet you; my name is Marlyn Olsen."

"I'm the office manager and don't usually do interviews, but we're short on help today. Follow me to my office. So you're an Olsen; sounds Scandinavian to me."

"I'm half Norwegian and . . ."

"I'll excuse that. I'm full-blooded Swede myself." He laughed as he leaned forward to study my application. "So you graded history papers and performed light office work in boarding school. In addition you worked in a library at college. Regrettably, Santa Monica is a closed market for clerical work, but there's an immediate opening in the policy department of an insurance company in downtown Los Angeles. I think you would qualify. Are you interested?"

"Sounds intriguing, but I don't have a car."

"No problem. There's a direct bus line. I'm acquainted with the head honcho that hires. Hold on, I'll make a call—You're on! It's an eight-to-five job and you start Monday morning. You'll report to Madge Turner."

"Keen! I'll give Mrs. Breckenridge a week's notice."

"Considering you're new in town, how about I drive you by the insurance company and then brief you on the bus line?"

City Jungle

My eyes fell on a nameplate on his desk. "Um—sure, Mr. Jensen."

"Call me Neal. I'll pick you up at five."

Crowded sidewalks with hurrying people edged every skyscraper in Los Angeles. Masses of taxis and buses crammed the streets. "It's rush hour. Don't sweat the noise. You'll get used to it. Here we are. Get off the bus at Eighth Street, walk half a block to the high-rise with the glass windows. That's your new office." He winked.

A joyride through Beverly Hills in Neal's convertible sports car ended up in a neighborhood of beautiful homes. "That's my house. I need to scoot in. Come on in. I'll be but a minute."

Standing in the living room behind a white leather couch, admiring a marble fireplace, I glanced toward the hall. My jaw dropped—the man appeared, stark naked! Flabbergasted, I shifted to the opposite side of the couch. He edged forward, a moronic grin on his face. My gaze flickered to the front door—a way to escape! No way will he go outdoors like that! Standing by his car, I pondered, *I'm penniless—no way to call my aunt, but I can outrun him if he dares to try anything.* In a short time he emerged fully dressed. "Get with it, little girl—this is the city, not Weimar! Jump in the car—I'll drive you back!" He didn't speak another word.

"Well, uh, um, sir. Thank you for the ride and the job."

Monday morning I showed up at the insurance company, and they were expecting me. Nothing was said about that incident. A pleasant surprise came when I found out the employment agency wrote off their take of my wages. As I gleaned that experience, I wondered how many girls this man had hoodwinked. Was I the first one to stand up to him? I never found out. *Lesson learned—never accept a ride (or a date) with a stranger no matter how well dressed or decent he looks.*

Later, when I told the story to my aunt, she chortled, "You taught that man a lesson, but remember—your dad has a special connection with God. You can be sure his prayers are being answered." *In the midst of strange situations, as in Psalm 139, I was not alone. God was not distant. He always showed up! I could count on that.*

I lived with Aunt Alice until my first paycheck. She helped me find a studio apartment only five blocks from where I worked, making it possible for me to walk to my employment. I earned exactly enough to pay rent, utilities, and food, with a few dollars left over. My aunt insisted I needed a phone for safety reasons, and paid to have it installed. For the

Beyond Ashes

first time in my life, I was supporting myself. I felt terribly grown up.

"Being brave means to know something is scary, difficult, and dangerous, and doing it anyway, because the possibility of winning the fight is worth the chance of losing it."[1]

---

1. Emilie Autumn, "Emilie Autumn Quotes," BrainyQuote.com, Xplore Inc, 2018, accessed February 20, 2018, https://www.brainyquote.com/quotes/emilie_autumn_448245.

CHAPTER 18

Three Surprise Visits

"Hi, Marlyn. I happen to be a couple of blocks from where you live. There's an Italian restaurant nearby. Are you interested?"

"Mike? What in the world? I haven't heard your voice in a coon's age! How are you?"

"Hungry as a bear coming out of hibernation, and I know you like Italian cuisine. How about it?"

"I'll be ready in a jiffy." Aunt Alice had met Mike at college when she picked me up. Apparently, she felt safe giving him my phone number.

Subsequent to a delicious meal and a few catch-up sentences, Mike leaned forward. "Say—it's Saturday night. The evening is young. I'm staying at the hotel across the street. Have you ever played poker?"

"I've tried it a couple of times just for fun—never for money. Not good at it."

"No money involved, and it's not as hard as you think. I'll teach you."

After we got started on the game, I discovered Mike had a particular version in mind—strip poker. *Oh boy, does this guy need to learn a lesson.* I determined I would do something to disrupt the game, but first appear to go along with it. Wearing a tank top under my blouse, I went as far as removing my blouse, but then abruptly stopped the game. "That's as far as this game goes! I know what you're up to! How dare you insult me!"

"There's buzz going around campus since you were expelled. Uh, I can see now it was all a lie. I'm chagrined beyond words. All I can say is I'm sorry, Marlyn." He flinched and paused. "I'm confused about life right now. Can we talk?"

"Sure, why not?"

"I know you're right about God. But me? I'm searching. I have to find my own answers. I'm not at the point in life where I deserve a good woman like you. I'll admit I admire your high ideals, but I'm not there yet. But I want you to know you are the most incredible woman I've ever met, and I don't want it to end like this. After my shenanigan, can we still be friends?"

"Yes, Mike, I'd like that."

Later that year, I received an invitation to attend Thanksgiving dinner at Mike's house. After a pleasant visit with his parents, Mike took me for a ride. Under the light of the moon, we chatted. "Marlyn, in addition to my goal in the medical field, I want to find a woman like you—once I mature, that is." He was a perfect gentleman the entire visit. That was the last time I saw Mike. I learned later that he successfully entered the field of radiology, married a psychologist, and was a family man to three children.

Silas?

A knock on the door and there Silas stood. "How in the world did you find me?"

"Don't you know? I'm a private eye." Tongue-in-cheek humor was written all over his face. "By the way, I've brought a couple friends." He revealed a bottle of vodka and 7UP. "Got any lemons?"

"You can come in, but not that stuff!"

"OK, Miss High-and-Mighty. I didn't drink at La Sierra, but I learned how to drink in the army. Life has been the pits since I left college. I didn't ace my finals, and the old man has disowned me. How would you feel if your dad disowned you?"

"My dad's not like that! He stood by me even when I was expelled. He called the dean and gave him a piece of his mind!"

"Do you have any idea how lucky you are?"

Sorrow flooded my soul for this man. He looked sad and in need of a friend. "Once a friend, always a friend—OK, Silas, you can come in."

"Life hasn't been that great for you either since you left. And Marlyn, what happened to your dreams? Here you are in a tiny apartment, living in the city jungle. Did being uppity get you anywhere? I don't see much difference between you and me. We're both losers." He mixed a drink and set it in front of me.

"I don't drink."

"One drink won't hurt you."

One drink led to another. Not used to drinking, my stomach revolted

Three Surprise Visits

and I vomited over and over. I was glad the next morning that it was Sunday and I didn't have to go to work, my head hurt so bad. I vowed never to drink again.

Lord, it's not easy to face hostile and opposing voices and still do what my heart tells me to do. Teach me how.

Even on the days we feel the most unlovable—God loves us still. Soon He would answer my prayer.

Timely visit

Two days later, Daddy stood on my doorstep. Joy and dread flooded over me as I instinctively wondered whether he would give me a lecture. Tiny earrings felt like giant pendulums. Red toenail polish matching my lipstick glared up at me. Daddy had always been strict about such things.

"Aren't you going to invite your dad in?" He smiled from ear to ear.

"Yes! Yes, of course!" I gasped with astonishment. "You're the best visitor I've had all week!" I grabbed his hand and pulled him in.

Daddy never said a word about my appearance. He glanced at the philosophy books in my small library. "Marlyn, as I've said before, we're cut from the same cloth! Those were my textbooks when I was your age. I'm elated to see your Bible, though. Still the best Book ever written." He grinned.

"I'm trying not to let it grow dust, but I've been so busy—what with my job and all."

"I want to hear all about your job, but first sit down and allow me to tell you a story. As you know, my mother died in my arms of a heart attack when I was nineteen. Eight motherless children she left behind, of which I was the second oldest. It shattered my heart. Another tragedy occurred when our dad took to drinking after she died and deserted the family. He took off for Seattle. I became a cowboy for several years, taming wild horses, drinking in saloons, participating in rodeos. I'd bring the money I earned home to help provide for my younger siblings. *I'm good enough on my own*, I thought. *Who needs God?* So I turned against Him."

"What happened then, Daddy?"

"A few years later, I remembered my promise to Mama before she died, that I'd go on to college. First I farmed out my younger siblings into good homes and then moved to San Francisco with plans to enroll in law school and become rich. While attending evangelistic tent meetings, I found the Lord again. God picked me up and set me on a mountaintop. He miraculously changed my path and opened the door for me to go to Southwestern College in Texas. While there I received a call to go to Mexico for mission service. I met your mother and it was love at first sight! She was the most beautiful woman I had ever met. When we married, I tried to change her to be what I thought she should be as a minister's wife. I was wrong to do that. I realize now I'd been too controlling. Your mother left me for good reasons. After the death of our beloved Milton, I tried to rush her along with the grieving process. Then when you kids left home she suffered badly from empty-nest syndrome."

"Oh, I'm so sorry, Daddy."

"Then the menopause smacked her like a ton of bricks. The house haunted her with memories. She loves you children so. She couldn't take it any longer and left home to live in the nurses' boarding house at the sanitarium." Daddy leaned forward, cupping a hand to his chin, and then looked up. "Your mother is a good woman. It was needed time for her to be alone and sort out all the hurts." He reached out and held my hands. "Marlyn, my dear child, I'm sorry for the hurt it heaped upon you, but the separation has been good for Mother and me. She's only a mile away. We stay in touch every day."

"I'm so glad. Tell me more."

"I've been pleading with God, and He has revealed areas in my life where I've been wrong—I've made things right between us." Daddy blanketed my hands in his. "Marlyn, I'm sorry, for the stress all this has caused you. I feel partly to blame for what happened to you at college. I beg forgiveness."

"Of course, Daddy, but, it wasn't your fault. I just didn't understand, and I allowed it to get the best of me."

"The good news is that your mother and I are working on a plan to get together again. We have plans that we are not ready to disclose, but it involves getting you back into college."

For three wonderful days I had Daddy all to myself. We shared many stories. His openness and honesty melted my heart. At times tears were shed between us, and a bond formed like never before. When it came time for him to leave, he said, "My precious daughter, you are as lovely as your mother, both inside and out. We love you very much. Please be careful in the big city. If you have a fault, it's that you are too trusting. Be on

Three Surprise Visits

guard. Your mom still worries about you, but remember you are covered in prayer. Nothing can happen to you without the Lord intervening."

"A visual is tucked in my heart of you kneeling at your chair, praying, Daddy."

My heart leaped with love for my parents. Daddy looked the handsomest he had looked since before the fire. There was renewed vigor in his voice. Scars were still on his face, but with new meaning. He had emerged from pain and suffering, stronger and more resilient. His scars were beautiful! I thought about how much my parents had sacrificed for their children—how much they loved us. Daddy's visit came exactly when I needed it. I had revived hope. I vowed in my heart not to let him or Mama down. I would move on.

"The soul would have no rainbow had the eyes no tears. Our tears are to be cleansing showers, not an endless flood" (John Vance Cheney).

CHAPTER 19

Four Close Calls

It was one of those picture-perfect days when you just have to get outside. When Darrell, a friend from work, called with an invitation, I was primed for it. "My brother-in-law, Pete, just got a new speedboat, and we were wondering if you would like to go with us to Catalina Island for the day."

"Would I? I'd love to!" I could hardly believe my good fortune.

We met Pete down at the harbor and climbed into a small inboard motorboat with two rows of seats. After securing our life jackets, we set off. The ocean was calm and sparkly, providing a smooth twenty-two-mile ride to Catalina. The island had been turned into a tourist destination, and we enjoyed exploring the town and island environs.

The return trip started as it had begun, but suddenly the wind picked up and the sea became turbulent. Gigantic waves towered over the boat, threatening to engulf it!

Pete looked grim as he gripped the steering wheel with naked fingers. "Darrell, get that bucket back there and start bailing water!"

The small boat heaved and tossed, thrashed about by the raging sea. The angry Pacific seemed assured of its prey, and the mainland looked a long way off.

Pete tried to head into the waves as much as possible to keep from being flipped over. Terrifying waves drenched our bodies as Darrell bailed water. We were thankful for our life jackets, but terrified about getting through the storm. Time seemed suspended.

The longer the storm raged, the more I froze in fear. I thought I was going to die. "Lord, help!" I cried over and over—my words whipped away by the howling wind. God heard my cries. He calmed the storm to a whisper, and the waves were hushed. Peace was in that stillness as God brought us safely to harbor.

Beyond Ashes

"Our situation may be full of trouble; emotions may be at war within us. Suddenly there is a mysterious peace, a peace that comes with healing in its wings, even the peace of God. Such moments remind us that beneath the raging tumult of even the perfect storm, there are the still waters of the ocean's depths."[1]

Midnight strangler?

From my vantage point in the lunchroom, sunlight drifted in through the window. The concrete jungle came alive as thousands of tiny windows on high-rise buildings looked like a million sparkling diamonds. A palm tree stood here and there. Mary, a typist in my department, sat at my table. "Marlyn, I know how hard it is for a single person to make ends meet. We're at the end of the month. Why don't you move in with me? I live in Long Beach. I have a car. It's a thirty-minute drive. By splitting the rent and utilities, we can cut our expenses in half."

"Long Beach? How close are you to the beach?"

"Four blocks."

"I'm move-in ready, but like how soon?"

"I can pick you up Sunday."

In her thirties, Mary was mom to half the people on the block—a caregiver to strays, hippies, and ex-druggies. Everyone was welcome. *Absolutely no drugs* was her maxim. Some came to chat, others for food. I was home alone the day after I arrived when a young girl knocked at the door. "Hi, my name is Katrina. Is Mary home?"

"No. She's at her boyfriend's. Do you know where that is?"

"No. I haven't eaten all day. I'm hungry. Is it OK if I wait for her?"

"Come in. I'll fix you a sandwich."

"I'm seventeen. I mostly live on the streets. My mother is an alcoholic and abusive. My childhood and past have been horrendous. I've lost count of how many times I've been raped by her boyfriends."

My heart ached for this girl. How I longed to help her. As I listened to her story, a severe headache developed. "I've got to run next door to the drugstore and pick up something for a headache."

"Like Excedrin?" Katrina dug in her purse and handed me two white tablets. "Here, this will clear your head." I swallowed the pills. The girl left. Thirty minutes later, I was as nervous as a canary in a cage with cats. I knew it was not Excedrin.

Four Close Calls

Soon Mary arrived. "Marlyn, I should've warned you. Katrina is new around here. She thought she was doing you a favor, but you can't trust her. I haven't had a chance to set her straight, and it's probably some kind of speed. I was once on methamphetamines and a few other unmentionables. Kind people reached out and helped me. Otherwise I might still be on the streets. I'm returning the favor by taking these kids in. I tell you what—you'll calm down if you jump in a tub of hot water and sweat it out."

As I soaked, I had second thoughts about my new home, but I felt compassion for these vagabonds. *Maybe that's why I'm here—to help Mary.*

After the incident, Mary introduced me to Chuckie and Jamey, two young fellows who lived in the apartment upstairs. "I'm assigning them to be your bodyguards. If I'm not around, just call on them." They were big strapping dudes from the hills of Tennessee and spoke with a southern drawl. It seemed like a new language. I liked that even though I was younger, they respectfully called me "ma'am."

A couple days later, Mary's friend Wayne stopped by, bringing a friend. "Meet Kip. He's my skydiving buddy. We're headed for the desert to go on a jump. You gals want to come along?"

"Not interested," Mary replied.

"Well then, how about your friend?" He looked at me.

"I'm fascinated with skydiving! Is it hard?"

"Nah, nothing to it. All you do is jump out and pull the rip cord. The parachute does the rest." Kip laughed a belly-rolling laugh.

"OK, Marlyn, if you want to go, go—but Wayne, I'm counting on you to look out for her. She's just a kid. I'll hold you responsible if anything happens."

Soon we were up in the plane, preparing to jump, my parachute securely fastened. The guys dove headfirst, arms spread out, turning somersaults in the sky. It was obvious they were not amateurs. Earth below looked like a bottomless pit. I hesitated. The thought flashed through my mind of the promise I had made to Mama about being cautious.

"Have you done this before?" the pilot shouted.

"Never."

"Don't jump!" He spoke forcefully. "These guys are experts. I can't believe they expected you to jump without training! Besides, Kip's a smart aleck! I wouldn't trust him if I were you."

Beyond Ashes

Just what I needed to hear, but after all the hype about jumping, I knew I'd take flak. Kip, who had paid for my parachute rental, was miffed. Back at the apartment, he laid into me. "OK, it's payback, baby girl," he yelled, and began to get fresh. I pushed him away. He slammed me against the wall. Pain shot through my shoulder.

"Leave her be," Wayne yelled, drawing a fist. "You mess with Mary's friends—you'll answer to me."

I was beginning to feel more and more out of place in this new environment. That idea was reinforced by an even more dangerous incident that followed the next day.

Mary needed to earn extra money and took on a part-time job on weekends—a barmaid at the Happy Hour Cocktail Lounge a block down the street. "Marlyn, you look depressed. It's Saturday night. Come down to the bar. Chuckie and Jamey will be there to guard you. You'll be safer there than here."

After Mary left, I was dubious about being alone. What if Kip showed up? I wandered to the bar.

"You look like you need a pick-me-up." Mary, always cognizant of others' emotional status, handed me a cocktail. "Don't worry. It's mild. Drink it. You'll feel better."

Sitting near the entrance, my back to the door, I cautiously sipped the drink through a straw. A stir in the center of the bar drew my attention. An older woman, perhaps about sixty-five, was stripping off her clothes while the patrons of the bar cheered and tossed her money.

Mary explained, "Sal used to be a stripper, and everyone in the neighborhood feels sorry for her. She comes in once a week. It's her means of earning money for food." *What a miserable life*, I thought.

Suddenly everything went black. The next thing I knew, I was back in my apartment, Chuckie gently slapping and pinching my face. "Wake up, Marlyn, drink this coffee."

"What, what happened?"

"Well, it's like I looked over to where you'd been sittin', and you was nowhere in sight. I hollered, 'Mary, where'd she go? She was sittin' there a minute ago!'

" 'I don't know,' Mary replied. 'Maybe she's left. It's past midnight. Run out and find her!' Jamey and I raced out to the parkin' lot," Chuckie explained. "This humongous guy was stuffing you into the back seat of his car. Jamey grabbed him while I snatched you out of the car. The man tore away from Jamey's grip."

"Yeah," Jamey added, "but not before I landed a good one on his jaw." Jamey punched the air. "He sped away wheels a-spinnin' something fierce—I tell you!"

Chuckie held the coffee to my lips. "Here, sip this. It's obvious he snuck something into your drink that knocked you out cold. We got to you just in time. Reckon you are one lucky chick! I ain't never seen anything like it before!"

"Who was it?" I gasped.

"Nobody knows. He was dressed kinda city folk-like and drove a new Buick. I ain't aiming to scare you, but we figure he might've been in the sex-slave market, or was maybe the midnight strangler. It's been in the L.A. papers!"

I gasped! The thought sent shivers down my spine. One thing struck me—*Daddy's prayers certainly are effective!*

Word of the incident got around. The owner of the bar approached me. "Marlyn, I've heard of your frightful experience. Mary's a good girl. She takes care of everybody around here. She's street smart and has a handle on things. Not you, and I don't blame you for what happened, but it's obvious you're out of place here. Naïveté is written all over your face, making you easy target for the bad guys. They'll find you. Get out while the gettin' is good. I'm going to tell you something I tell my daughter—get yourself back in college and make something of yourself!"

I felt flawed and imperfect, yet I felt drenched in the grace and mercy that is found in Jesus Christ. Happy to be alive, I didn't hesitate to get out. I found a studio apartment west of the insurance company. It was farther to walk to work, but in a better neighborhood, and nearby stood a fire station. I felt safer, but nonetheless, every night I barricaded a chair against the door. When I wrote home to Mama, I didn't tell her about the near-abduction. I knew it would frighten her.

A new focus

"Marlyn, I need to talk to you." Mrs. Turner motioned me into her office and gestured toward a chair. I wondered what was so important that she needed to have a private talk with me. "I've wanted to say this for a long time. I really appreciate your work. You're the best I have. You do twice as many policies as anyone else. Your work is careful—even perfect. So I say this with reluctance. I would hate to lose you, but you should know there is a great job opening upstairs in the elite underwriting department. You would be working collaboratively with the Marine Underwriting Team. The job entails reviewing, underwriting, and rating, and preparing comprehensive boat insurance, from small boats to mega-yachts, for both private parties and boating companies. Since it's a training position, you might even consider making it a career. In addition, there's great opportunity for salary advancement. I know Mr. Bennett, the supervisor. I have already given him a high recommendation for you. He wants to see you for an interview tomorrow. You're a sharp dresser, but be sure to put on your best professional outfit and give it your best shot. Good luck."

"Thank you so much. I deeply appreciate your interest in me."

The next day, after completing both the verbal and written parts of the interview process, I got the position. The underwriters were professional and friendly. I set my heart into the work and began to think of what Mrs. Turner had hinted—if I couldn't get back to college, perhaps I could indeed make this a career. My life had a new focus, and I began to feel like I was getting somewhere.

Walking to work each day, I passed by a fire station. The fire chief, a man in his fifties, would often stop what he was doing to chat with me. "I have a daughter your age, and I like you. I'll watch out for you and be sure you're safe as you walk to and from work each day."

One day he questioned, "Marlyn, are you really happy at work? Do you have money left over to set aside for your college education? I know that's your real goal. You'd make a fine schoolteacher."

"I like the work, but I don't really have much to show for it after the usual expenses. However, I'm due for pay raises as the job progresses."

"Well, I have a suggestion you can't pass up. You should try part-time modeling. A lot of girls work their way through college that way. I have connections and could get everything set up for you. What do you say?"

The idea of earning extra money and getting back in college sounded appealing. "Sure, it's worth a try." I visualized modeling elegant clothes for a catalog company.

"OK, I'll set up an appointment for a professional photographer to come over to your apartment for a photo shoot."

Sure enough, a photographer showed up with his crew. "I think you'll

Four Close Calls

fill the bill. Here's what I want you to wear." The "clothes" were next-to-nothing—in fact, downright scandalous. My innate sense of modesty kicked in, and I refused to wear them.

The photographer didn't look happy. "Look, if you really want to get into the modeling business and make *big bucks*, you're going to have to learn to cooperate. Modesty is not an issue in this game. Here's my card. If you change your mind, let me know." He left, and with him, my potential modeling career. The photo shoot was a fiasco, but I knew I had made the right decision. But then an event occurred that would change my life forever.

---

1. Charles Henderson.

CHAPTER 20

I'm That Girl

The doorbell startled me awake. One o'clock in the morning? After the third ring I got up and peered through the peephole. Silas? Leaving the chain guard intact, I opened the door a crack. "What are you doing here at this unearthly hour?"

"Please let me in. I need to talk." Though groggy, I opened the door—I hadn't seen him for a while, but I still felt a soft spot in my heart for Silas. He barged in, alcohol on his breath.

"I want to turn my life around. You're the only one that understands me."

"Booze will get you nowhere." I yawned and stretched.

"You're right. I need your help."

It's hard to describe the next moments. I had let Silas in because we were friends. Straightaway it seemed he had an agenda. I said No, No, and No! Then suddenly it was happening.

As he left, Silas tried to justify his actions. "Don't worry about getting pregnant. While I was in the army, one of my parachute jumps didn't open up as it should, and I landed in some trees. As a result, I'm sterile—so, no babies ever for me."

Self-incriminating thoughts overwhelmed me. *Why did I let him in? Why couldn't I have resisted more? What if his sterility story isn't true?* Mostly I hit mental walls, but echoing in the cognitive part of my brain was the assurance—*I said NO!* Too late I realized the shattering truth—*I had been used by a trusted friend.* But my job was my lifeline. In the morning I went to work; grieving was put on hold.

Later, despite my incessant praying, the test strip showed positive. *Why, oh God, why?* My world spiraled downward. *I'm single, alone, and afraid. What am I going to say to my parents, my employers, and Silas?* I attempted to keep calm and composed, but really didn't know how to deal with what seemed unresolvable.

Beyond Ashes

I located Silas. "You're not sterile. The doctor confirmed that I'm pregnant."

"There's no way I can help you. I was high—you could've stopped me. I don't have a job. You'll have to deal with this yourself. You have options, if you know what I mean."

I said NO—he didn't respect my wishes. Alone, scared, worn down, and fighting defeat, I wrestled with negative self-talk. How could this have happened? *Why, oh why, God, did You allow this? Why are You allowing a child into this world through me, by a guy who doesn't even care? I don't understand. I've made mistakes, but my whole life I've tried to do the right thing—to be the good girl. Here I am, unmarried and pregnant.* Before me was a world that didn't make sense. Though emotions tangled deeply, survival mode kicked in. I managed to go to work each day, eat healthy meals, and go on long walks to keep my weight down.

Whom can I talk to? Aunt Alice had a boyfriend now who was taking up all her time. *I don't want to bother her.* Somehow my parents would have to know, but living hundreds of miles away, I couldn't face them with the news directly, not even over the phone.

Marlene, a neighbor, stopped by. "Marlyn, you're not yourself. What's going on?"

"I'm pregnant." So I told her the story.

"I'd understand if you had an abortion."

My stomach churned. "I can't. No matter how awful I feel—a baby's life is not mine to take. An abortion is not an option."

In the middle of the second trimester, about sixteen weeks, I felt the tiny life inside me. Every time I felt the flicker, my heart leaped—I fell in love! The doctor said the baby weighed about three and a half ounces, and was a little longer than a peapod. He talked about my options: either keep the baby and raise it as a single mom, or adoption. I thought about adoption, but I couldn't reconcile with the idea. I couldn't imagine giving part of myself to a stranger. I had just turned twenty-one. "I'm the baby's mama. I will keep this baby."

A blessing was hidden in the struggle I faced. I had to be willing to open my heart and mind to see it. As I got further along, I began to feel the baby moving inside. I remembered how I had felt at the wonder of Milton moving around in Mama's belly. I became excited to meet this little angel! *Life is incredible, and then it's awful. And then it's incredible again*. At the doctor's office, I heard the heartbeat—a life growing inside me—a life breathtakingly beautiful. For the first time in months of anxiety and turmoil—in the midst of my brokenness—I felt overwhelming peace and courage. No matter how scared I was, this baby was mine to keep.

Family

My sister Millie, a student now at an academy in Southern California, was a godsend. She would spend her home leave with me. We had enjoyed a shared comradeship, an esprit de corps, many times in our childhood. I cherished her visits. The first in the family to learn about my pregnancy, she offered hope and comfort. She would pat my belly and sing, "I am your auntie. I love you. I hope you are a girl."

Her enthusiasm was catching. I'd chime in, "I am your mommy. I love you, and I hope you are a girl." Thus Millie and I bonded even more deeply.

When Mama called to announce that her long-anticipated visit was in the offing, I was ecstatic, but nonetheless jittery. Barely showing at six months, I knew the time had come to tell her. I wondered how she would react.

Mama's sixth sense caught on before I could tell her. Placing a hand on my belly, she questioned, "Tell me, daughter—are you with child?" *Mama's taking this so calmly—I wonder if Millie has prepared her.* As I spilled out the story, Mama gently embraced me and rocked me in her arms.

"Mama, I'm scared out of my wits about how I'm going to handle this, but I've thought it through. I want to keep my baby."

"Of course, my child, I would have it no other way. You have my full support. I will love this baby as much as I love you." Mama's assuring love and approval provided a quantum leap for my morale.

"I'm hesitant about telling Daddy. What will he say?"

"Your daddy appreciates honesty. The best thing you can do is to tell him." She handed me the phone.

"Daddy, I have news that might be difficult for you to take. Please sit down." I paused, breathing in deeply. "Daddy—I, I'm six months pregnant."

"What? I'm trying to absorb what you just said. Did . . . you . . . just . . . say . . . you . . . are . . . pregnant?"

"Yes, Daddy. I feel like I've disappointed you so much lately. You've

Beyond Ashes

had such high hopes for me to get back into college."

"I'll admit I wasn't expecting this."

"Daddy, I'm too choked up to talk right now. Is it OK if Mama gives you the details?"

"Of course, but I'm glad you had the courage to tell me. I will have a lot of questions. For now, I want you to dry your tears and focus on being strong—for yourself, and for the baby. I promise to get back with you soon."

Two days later a letter came in the mail from Daddy. It displayed not a hint of, "How could you have done this?" Instead it demonstrated love and encouragement. At the bottom, a postscript brought a smile to my face. "You can count on me. I'll be down in a few days to support you and the baby in any way I can."

A week later Daddy arrived with gifts: maternity clothes from Mama and a book on childbirth. "I'm here for you. I want to know everything. Tell me about the father of this baby."

"His name is Silas Schmidt. Remember? He's the one I dated at college. His father is a business administrator for a university in Los Angeles, and quite adept at taking charge. He's adamant that I give up my baby for adoption. He's even gone as far as finding adoptive parents. He describes them to be quite wealthy."

"He did, did he—well, let me see what I can do."

Daddy arranged to meet with Mr. Schmidt and Silas.

"Mr. Olsen, I'm glad you arranged this meeting. Perhaps you can help me talk with your daughter. She's behaving inadvisably."

They talked back and forth for a while. As I listened to them air the pros and cons, inside I glowed that Daddy could so ably stand up for me. "Mr. Schmidt, clearly it is a fact that my daughter's situation was not of her choosing. She has given it much thought. Bottom line—she's twenty-one years old, a responsible young lady, and quite capable of making her own resolutions. Her mother and I support her one hundred percent in her decision to keep this baby."

Refusing to take "No" for an answer, Mr. Schmidt continued to spew out his ideas in no uncertain terms. Red-faced, Daddy stood up, his fists clenched. Closing his eyes briefly to whisper a prayer, Daddy regained his composure, stating firmly, "As far as my daughter and I are concerned, the case is settled and this meeting is adjourned." When he offered to

I'm That Girl

shake Mr. Schmidt's hand, it was refused.

In the parking lot, Daddy turned to Silas. "Young man, it's about time for you to grow up and learn to take responsibility."

Silas, who had remained silent throughout the meeting, walked over to me and whispered, "Have you any idea how lucky you are to have a father like that? My dad has done nothing but berate me. You know, I was actually glad to see your dad stand up to him. And your dad's right, I have the emotional mentality of a twelve-year-old, but I don't expect you could understand that."

I had harbored ill feelings toward Silas. At that moment I felt sorry for him. Everything he had disclosed to me about his father was true. No wonder he'd had problems growing up.

I followed Daddy's advice to take Silas to court to establish paternity and to petition for child support. In an attempt to deny that Silas was the father, Mr. Schmidt had hired an attorney. A blood test showed a perfect match. The judge saw the evidence. Looking at my baby, who was three months old, and then at Silas, the judge declared, "Look at her, Silas; why, this baby looks just like you! Of course she's yours! My judgment is sixty dollars a month child support for two years, after which the case will be reconsidered. Case dismissed."

For two years I received a monthly check from Mr. Schmidt, after which I sent a card of thanks for sending the child support money, and a note to let him know I would not be renewing the case. Included was a picture of my daughter.

I'm that girl that got pregnant. Sometimes a difficult situation brings people closer and strengthens their bonds. In my case it did. In this challenging situation, my family gave me unconditional love, support, kindness, forgiveness, acceptance, teamwork, and optimism for the future.

And there was God. He didn't look at my frazzled life and say, "OK, now you are on your own." He makes something good come out of everything. He gave me back double for what I had lost and blessed me with a beautiful baby daughter. I named her Laura Michelle. Laura means "crowned with laurels, symbolic of honor and victory." Michelle means "gift from God." The Creator of the universe took delight in her existence, and sang a song of joy. *"This child will be strong. She will have a special place in the world. She will bless many people with her strength."* My baby was a princess, a gift from God.

Beyond Ashes

Dear reader:

If you or someone you know has been in a similar situation and don't know where to turn—*you matter*. Your experience may not be like mine, and that's OK. Your experience, whatever it looks like—your decision, whatever you make—matters. It may be you don't have a strong support system, but there is hope in the One who created you. God is sheer mercy, rich in love. He puts victims back on their feet. He makes everything come out right. There is hope for you. There is hope for your child. You do not have to go through this alone. You can live a life of victory even in this crazy world. My heart cries with you for the tears you may shed. As I write this, I'm thinking of you. Please know that my prayers are with you.

CHAPTER 21

"Daddy, Wake Up!"

When Aunt Alice purchased a new home in Tarzana, she invited me to help her start a day care center. Midpoint in working on a layout plan, I got a letter from Daddy. "Our homestead in Weimar is up for sale with a potential buyer. Game plan is to relocate near a Christian college where you can continue with your education. Your mother and I will assist you in raising Lori. At the same time, Millie can finish high school and then pursue a nursing degree. Enclosed is a plane ticket for you to fly home for Thanksgiving, when we can discuss the plan."

Intrigued by what seemed to be a new adventure, I pondered the idea. *What about my commitment to Aunt Alice? How will she react?* Aunt Alice had often been my mentor. We were kindred spirits.

She held my hands and looked into my eyes. "I would like nothing better than to keep you and Lori, but you can't overlook a good opportunity. I know how much your daddy wants you to finish college. I'm sure you will want to explore this idea."

"Auntie, I'm torn betwixt and between. I'll admit it sounds intriguing, but I also like the idea of being a stay-at-home mama for my baby. I'm good with children, and I like the idea of helping you with this project."

"Marlyn, it's a decision only you can make, and I won't hold you back. Whatever you decide, remember, you'll always have a home here with me."

Thanksgiving Day dawned gray and cold. Keyed up with the possibility of rosy prospects, I arrived home. Lori, a loving and energetic child at three months old, was snug in my arms. At last I could introduce her to family. I knew they would love her at first sight! Millie immediately engulfed Lori in her arms and smothered her with kisses—a memory I'll always cherish.

Beyond Ashes

"Why is it so quiet? Where is everyone?"

"Mama's working the afternoon shift. Daddy's been in a clinic in Auburn. He'll be home soon. We'll feast tomorrow at Wanda's for Thanksgiving, a banquet to be sure!"

"Can't wait! Sis is the best cook in the state—my mouth waters just thinking about it!"

"Me too—she's fixing our favorites!"

At that moment Daddy's car pulled up in the driveway. I ran outside. "What's going on, Daddy? Why were you at the clinic?"

"Put a smile on your face and hug your daddy. I'm just fine." Reaching out for Lori, he chortled, "I'm especially fine now! My, what a pretty little girl you are." He carried her inside to his favorite rocking chair, sat down, and plopped her on his lap. Lori patted his cheeks and pulled on his moustache.

"This child is blonde and blue-eyed. Why, I believe she favors my side of the family. My little Norwegian lass, you look like your great-auntie Clara when she was a tyke. Look, she's tugging at my wrist, ready to take my pulse. A born nurse you are." And so the prattle went on between them.

"Daddy, I love how you two have hit it off, but it's time to feed her. I promise you can hold her again in just a bit."

"I'm so glad you are nursing her. Your mama nursed all five of you. I'll go into the kitchen and make fresh carrot juice. It's delicious, and grandbaby will get it secondhand." He winked.

With a full belly, Lori smacked her lips and burped contentedly. I kissed her plump cheeks. "Come, baby girl, Grandpapa is waiting!" Cradling her in my arms, I walked into the living room to see Daddy kneeling at his favorite chair praying, his open Bible before him—a scene I had seen many times in my life. Daddy loved his Bible, and he loved to pray. I knew he was praying for his family, each one by name. I tiptoed out of the room, a warm glow in my heart.

About ten minutes later, with Lori in my arms, I walked through the living room in search of Daddy. *Where is he? My stars! Why is Daddy lying on the kitchen floor?* Alarmed, I touched his cheek. His skin was cool and pale, his eyes wide open. No breath! No heartbeat! *No—it can't be!* Frantically, I yelled for Millie. "Millie, come quick!"

She knelt to the floor. "Daddy, Daddy, wake up!" Millie cried over and

"Daddy, Wake Up!"

over, "Please wake up!" But Daddy just lay there. Placing her face on his chest, she sobbed. In the midst of the agony of the situation, I'll never forget the peaceful look on Daddy's face, eyes wide open, as though he had looked into the face of Jesus before he took his last breath. I had seen death at the nursing home. I knew he was gone. Millie and I both knew. But I also knew the look of peace. Gently, Millie closed Daddy's eyelids.

I must call an ambulance! I must call Wanda! Next to the telephone I spotted Daddy's Bible, still on the chair where he had been praying. It was open to Revelation 21; verse 4 was highlighted: "And God shall wipe away all tears from their eyes; and there shall be no more death, neither sorrow, nor crying, neither shall there be any more pain: for the former things are passed away" (KJV). I wondered, *Did Daddy know he was going to die?* My heart got stuck in my throat, and my mind spun like a top. Adrenaline kicked in. I managed to call the emergency ward at the sanitarium.

"I'll send an ambulance right out and notify your mother," an impersonal voice replied. *Could this be real?*

The arrival of an ambulance bringing Mama, with Wanda right behind, released the emotions I had suppressed. I heard Mama tell the paramedics that earlier in the week a pain had begun in Daddy's chest. Thinking it was indigestion and heartburn, a chronic problem, he had checked himself into a clinic. "I was afraid it might be his heart, but he didn't think so," Mama sobbed. "He was too excited about our move."

Slight drizzle, as though heaven were weeping, is ingrained in my mind; with it, a blurred memory of huddling in a circle with Mama, Wanda, and Millie. Trembling, we watched paramedics cover Daddy with a blanket, load him on the stretcher, and then drive away. Punched in the gut, I thought, *Mama needs Daddy. Our whole family needs him. And what about our future plans?* Slobbery kisses watered my face, as though to kiss away the boo-boo. Motherly love surged through me. I held Lori tight in my arms. The love comforted me to the depth of my soul.

Later, an autopsy revealed that a myocardial rupture took Daddy's life—a heart attack as a result of a muscle tear that had begun four days earlier. At the clinic, that pain had been mistakenly diagnosed as heartburn and indigestion, and that's how he had been treated. But it indeed was a heart attack.

Beyond Ashes

Grief

The aftermath was the same blast of shock, grief, and paperwork that every family who has suddenly lost someone is stricken with. At the funeral, people came to pay tribute: family, church family, relatives from out of town—masses of people. Daddy was a friend to everyone: the postmaster, the grocer, merchants in Auburn as well as in Colfax, where he had helped start a church (now a thriving congregation). Multitudes showed up to pay respects to a man who was an encourager—warm, witty, and loving—a man who shared his love for the Lord in tangible ways, such as regularly helping a widow with twelve children. I learned I was not the only one who thought my daddy was incredible. I learned even more how much my daddy had cared about me. Countless strangers told me, "Your daddy loved you very, very much. He was so proud of you." The stories I heard and continue to hear about my dad have confirmed what I've known all along: Daddy was one of a kind—a man who touched many lives and would be missed by myriads of people.

The loss of a parent digs deeply, stings sharply, and alters your world in unimaginable ways. The first few weeks, the first few months, are a gloss-over of camouflaged sadness. Christmas was nearly unbearable. After a while, my siblings and I, and finally Mama, came to grips with what had happened. We picked ourselves up off the ground and started on the road back to normalcy. Lori was the ray of sunshine that illuminated my path. Truly a gift from God!

In Daddy's last breath my plans for college vanished. But college didn't seem that important. My mind and heart were wrapped around a bright-eyed baby daughter, my priceless treasure. My life took on new meaning: to be a good mother was my aspiration. Lori and I moved to Weimar to live near Mama. I found employment at the Weimar Sanitarium, where Mama, Frank, and Millie worked.

When Daddy died, our family lost a treasure beyond all imagining. He had been the backbone of our family—always positive, always encouraging. Personally, I didn't realize how much my faith had been riding on the shirttails of his faith. After his untimely death, I went through a season of feeling alone, abandoned by God. I couldn't wrap my mind around the unfairness of life. I couldn't come up with any answers. I was in spiritual distress, but not in spiritual failure, because God still loved me. In time I would know that. In time, He would grow in me a new capacity for a

"Daddy, Wake Up!"

relationship with Him—my own. But it was on hold for a while.

Daddy had left a legacy that I would come to appreciate. One is a treasured poem he had penned just for me. The original, in his handwriting, is tucked in my Bible, close to my heart.

A Message for You
I have a message for you now
The Savior soon will come.
I hope to reach your heart somehow
To find you there, in kingdom come.
The way is dark and rough and long.
With courage, strength, and fondest hope
Put on your boots with prayer and song.
With faith and love your problems cope.
You have a promise sweet and true,
You'll find it there in His dear Word.
Jesus gave His life for you,
The sweetest message you have heard.
Now walk the way with utmost care,
Take each step with careful aim.
You'll find the way with song and prayer,
And soon arrive in His dear name.
Monrad E. Olsen

Daddy, you didn't live long enough to see your message fulfilled in my heart. I found my way with prayer and song. I can't wait for the day I will wrap my arms around you and say, "Daddy, your sweet message reached my heart."

CHAPTER 22

A Turn in the Road

> It's a world of laughter, a world of tears
> It's a world of hopes and a world of fears
> There's so much that we share that it's time we're aware
> It's a small world after all [1]

This popular tune in the sixties became arguably the most-sung song in the world. The Cuban Missile Crisis and the Vietnam War gave rise to the song's message of a hope for peace and brotherhood. Far and wide tension mounted as the war escalated. Far and wide people longed for peace. Far and wide this song was translated into many languages. It is claimed that this song has been performed and translated more than any other piece of music.[2] It was estimated that, on Disney attractions alone, the song has played nearly fifty million times worldwide.[3]

I first heard the song at my workplace when a nurse played it on a radio, and it spoke to my heart. I wanted peace! But in America there was very little peace. Every day the news reported the names of American servicemen killed the previous day. *Would a son be drafted? Would a son be on the death list?* Daddy's untimely death had come as a tsunami just when I needed a tailwind. Reminders of him and Milton lurked everywhere. And my heart grieved with the multitudes who were losing loved ones. *God, where are You in this world of turmoil?* I questioned God, but I can't say I was seeking Him for an answer; still, God showed up in some of the most splendid ways.

I was assigned to the 3:00–11:00 P.M. work shift at Weimar Sanitarium, and my near-midnight walks back to the car would send shivers up and down my spine. Fear of the dark gripped my soul, an aftereffect of the dreadful night of the fire. On clear nights, the glow from the Milky Way, the Big Dipper, and the Pleiades star cluster eased the quaking.

Beyond Ashes

The eeriness on a certain black night is forever ingrained in my memory. A pitch-black curtain of clouds draped over the sky. Taunting images seemed to loom in the bushes, waiting to pounce on me. *God, I can't see You above the clouds. Where are You?* Instantly the moon appeared, like a celestial companion. I felt God's presence, His voice saturating my soul. *"Do not be afraid, My child. You are not alone. I am with you."* Tears forming at the corners of my eyes poured freely down my cheeks: tears I didn't want to push away. Not tears of sadness—no, tears of joy, tears of relief, tears of freedom, tears washing away my pain. Cool midnight air kissed my face, signaling a green light to climb out of the pit of fear, the beginning of releasing the old and embracing the new. I was a child of the Most High God! Future walks back to the car would be stamped with His promise of protection.

Lori is four months old. God, I'm going to church today. Will I be accepted as a single parent? Friendly people welcomed me with open arms, admiring my little daughter. I smiled, feeling at home in my own church again. Alas, that lasted but momentarily.

After church an old classmate asked if she could hold my baby. "Marlyn, it must be hard to be a single parent. My husband and I have talked it over. We've come up with a plan you can't possibly turn down. We want to adopt your baby. That way you can get back into college and the baby will have a mom and a dad." Smiling smugly, she clung to my baby and continued to warble, "And really, you must know, it would be best for everyone."

Sudden emotion triggered inside. *This woman is serious.* I grabbed my baby and fled to the car. *Are you kidding, lady? No way are you going to snatch my baby away from me!* The ploy wasn't over. The next day her mother-in-law, a staunch church leader, called Wanda. With condescending intonation she attempted to persuade my sister how much better off the baby would be in a two-parent home. I was most thankful Wanda stood up for me, and I shed tears of gratitude. Life had repeatedly disappointed me. I'd experienced many losses. *These people may be top brass in the church, but no way am I going to give up the love of my life. No other human being on planet earth could love my baby as much as I do.* Overwhelmed by the insensitivity of this family, my heart received a painful wound. It would be years before I would step foot in that church again.

Feeling overrun and frazzled, trying not to let it show, the truth is I was out of touch with my feelings. I wasn't sensitive enough to the things my mind and heart needed to nurture me in my brokenness. Inside I coddled a neat package of hurt feelings, and I didn't know how to rid myself of them. For a long time I secretly judged the woman and anyone who poked at my wounded self-confidence. Maturity in life experiences has no timing. It wasn't until later that I had a major breakthrough in my life, when I learned how to properly love myself, and all that changed. Countless physical miracles had already taken place in my life, miracles that made me realize God's presence. God was preparing me for a spiritual healing of heart, mind, and soul. First, I would need to learn the path of forgiveness. In time I would learn the freedom that comes with forgiving others, as well as the freedom that comes with forgiving oneself for wasted time. *God is not a God of the quick fix. Change, growth, and healing take time.*

Even so, a few loving people from my community of faith offered friendship. My parents had raised me to be positive. Hurt feelings or not, that's the road I would choose. With a smile on my face and a smile for my baby, I chose to walk in sunshine, to bask in my high calling as a mother, regardless of how some people might feel. In time I came to the resolution that people could make me feel bad only if I allowed them to.

News hot off the press!
"Marlyn, a tall handsome fella has just been hired. He's my grandson and you must meet him!" Papa Boles, as he was affectionately called, was one of the charge nurses and a respected friend of our family. His grandson had just finished a stint in the military. Indeed, Eric was handsome, six-foot-four, with dark wavy hair. Charmed by his happy-go-lucky disposition and good-natured humor, the patients and staff took to him right away. Soon the matchmaking began. Spring was in the air: *Why not?* We managed to work in a few dates. But because of conflicting work schedules, we had hardly any time to get acquainted. Still, the community soon began viewing us as an item.

A retired admiral in the navy, Papa Boles had been beating the drum for Eric to make the navy a career. "There's a great big world out there for you to explore. There's no future in this tiny town for either you or Marlyn. Why not propose and reenlist?"

"Wear your best dress; we're eating fancy tonight." It was Eric on the phone. After a filet mignon steak dinner at a fancy restaurant, I was smacked between the eyes with an unforeseen announcement. "Marlyn, I have something important to tell you. Selective Service has notified me that I have to report to the local draft board. Drafting means army or marines, but I've decided to jump the gun and have a say in the matter."

"What did you do?"

"I managed to pull a few strings and talk to the right people. Since I've already served four years in the navy, I've reenlisted. I served as a radioman. My records show I was a darned good one. I'll be stationed in San Diego for advanced training in that field. I adore you and your little daughter." He reached for my hands. "I'm not the most romantic guy in the world, but I can't stand the idea of not seeing you again. How about we make it permanent and get married? Lori needs a daddy. I helped raise my kid sister. I'd be good to your baby girl."

"I'm fond of you, Eric, but really I'm blown over. I don't know what to say. We've dated only two months."

"I don't expect an answer right away. A friend told me about some cottages for rent on Mission Beach."

"Mission Beach? I remember it from my girlhood days in National City—a gorgeous isthmus on the Pacific—the ocean on one side and the bay on the other!"

"You'd love it, then. I'll be leaving in two weeks to look it over. I'd like you to go with me. Think about it and let me know." Excitement was in his voice.

When I talked it over with Mama, it was apparent Eric had utterly charmed her. "He certainly is good-looking! If he's anything like Papa Boles, it would be hard to find a nicer fellow. I'm surprised you're jumping into something this quick, but certainly you have my blessing!"

My supervisor looked deep into my eyes. "You know, Marlyn, good men still exist. Eric is a good worker, well-mannered, and the patients adore him. I was married to a sailor once. There's a lot of perks in the military. If I were you I'd give it some thought. By the way, did you know Papa Boles is already calling you his granddaughter-in-law?" She winked.

Wanda's reaction was quick and to the point: "Is he a believer?"

"He believes there is a God, but he said his religious experience has been when Papa and Mama Boles took him to church, and when he visits his dad and step-mom in Atlanta. She's the minister of music at a large church. He's been to their church many times."

After about a week I neatly wrapped it up in my mind: *I've already compromised my strict religious upbringing. Eric believes in God. When I'm ready to get seriously back to God and church, I'm sure he'll join me. Moving to San Diego as a military wife seems like an adventure! And here is a chance to escape painful memories. My ten-month-old daughter will love the sea as much as I do.* I reveled in the idea of being a stay-at-home mom living by the sea—the sea being the deciding factor. A few days later, Eric and I were married in a small chapel in Reno, surrounded by family. I was a bit startled when his mom showed up apparently drunk. "She gets that way sometimes," was his explanation.

Beach home
A gem of a cottage on Mission Beach became our home—the location, surrounded by palm trees, made it a paradise. Eric's hours on the base were long; we didn't see much of each other. I'd get up before dawn to fix breakfast and would have a hot meal waiting for him when he arrived home late in the evening. When Eric had weekends off, he'd hoist Lori on his shoulders and we'd take off west for an evening stroll on the beach, or east to watch the dolphins frolic in the bay.

Abby, a navy wife who lived next door, and I were kindred spirits. Her daughter Samantha was the same age as Lori, and the two of them enjoyed many happy hours of playtime. The gentle waves of the bay made it our favorite go-to place. It fascinated our babies, wading in shallow water and playing merrily in the sand. For naptime, they'd sleep in a playpen shaded by a sun umbrella. At these times Abby and I talked about life, and sometimes we talked about God. We taught our little ones and other little children on the beach songs about Jesus, especially their favorite: "Jesus Loves Me." I have many happy memories of living on Mission Beach. Even though we didn't see much of each other, Eric and I enjoyed quality time together and were happy.

In no time at all I was pregnant. Eric was enchanted! He fancied the idea of having another child, and he hoped for a son. To our dismay he received orders that he would be deployed to Vietnam in the spring and that the ship was scheduled to leave on the very same day our baby was due to be born. No way did either of us want Eric to miss the birth of his child! In an effort to speed it up, we walked up and down the hills at the San Diego Zoo. Sure enough, a week before the due date, I went into labor at one thirty in the morning—and it was fast! "Get me there in a hurry! This baby is not going to wait!" I begged. We took off high speed for the hospital, only to find eight deliveries going on all at once, and only four doctors!

"No doctor available—you'll have to wait!" A steely-faced nurse decided to delay the birth by holding my legs together. I knew the baby would be born with the next contraction. I kicked her away just in time to watch my baby fight his way out of the birth canal. A doctor rushed in to deliver him.

Baby Ernie entered the world with a smile, a perfect little face with dimples. Right away his sunny personality reminded me of my little brother, Milton. How perfect to be a new mother again! In my arms I held a baby, another miracle created by an incredible God, a God who looked at him as a masterpiece. God sang another song: *"I will make this little one strong. He will cheer the world with his smile. He will be a lover of nature and animals, furry ones and creepy ones big and small. He will love the outdoors. He will be surrounded by children—his own as well as others."*

A week after Ernie was born, Eric was sent to Norfolk, Virginia. There, he would board the USS *Annapolis* escort carrier. Upon arrival off the coast of Vietnam, the *Annapolis* immediately began providing communications services between naval units and shore communication facilities. Eric was gone for an entire year—a year that brought many changes.

---

1. Richard M. Sherman and Robert B. Sherman, "It's a Small World (After All)." Lyrics taken from Lyrics.com, accessed February 22, 2018, https://www.lyrics.com/lyric/3103666/Disney/It%27s+a+Small+World+%28After+All%29.

2. "It's a Small World," Songfacts, accessed February 21, 2018, http://www.songfacts.com/detail.php?id=4691.

3. Richard Corliss, "Is *This* the Most Played Song in Music History?" *Time*, April 30, 2014, http://time.com/82493/its-a-small-world-50th-anniversary/.

CHAPTER 23

War Comes Home

Late afternoon sunshine peeked through fluffy clouds as I gazed out the window. The touch of gold in the array lifted my weariness. Lucy sat up on hind legs, her tail thumping the floor. Lori, who had just finished eating supper, broke off a piece of her cookie for the dog. I turned back toward the bassinet where Ernie lay sleeping. *Lori is eighteen months old, Ernie a newborn. Eric will be gone 365 days. I love my babies. I love my beach cottage. Lord, I know You are here. I see You shining through the clouds; yet I feel so all alone. What now?*

The phone rang. Wanda was on the other end. "Hi, sis; Mom's nerves are shot worrying about you and the babies living so far away. For real, so are mine. How about moving back?"

"I've been thinking about home, but where would we live?"

"As much as you like the ocean, would you settle for a creek?"

"A creek?"

"Just today a house came up for rent a mile from where I live, *and it's near a creek*. The house is perfect—just right for you and the kids. I've talked with the landlord, and he's willing to hold it for you."

A grin spread across my face. "I'm interested, and if you like the house I'm sure I'll like it too!" We chatted a few minutes. "I've got to run, sis; Ernie is waking up. I'll call you later for more details."

"I hear you, my little man. Auntie Wanda said your cousin Troy is all zipped up about having a boy cousin. I can't wait to show you off!" We joined Lori and Lucy, who were sitting on the porch swing gazing at the sky—gold, purple, amber, and crimson above the western horizon. Tears began trickling down my face at the beauty of the sunset, the most glorious I'd ever seen.

"Why you *cwy*? Mommy—*pwetty* sky."

"Mommies cry when they're happy, baby girl. Jesus painted a picture in the sky just for us." Feeling magnificently blessed, I held my babies tight. We rocked and sang, "With Jesus in the family, happy, happy home," to the rhythm of the porch swing. We weren't alone. Jesus was with us. He would make a way—and He did.

Later that evening Eric's aunt called, offering to drive down and help us get moved. The future looked promising.

Daffodils, a creek, and a dog

Within a short time, the children and I were in the embrace of loved ones. Adjusting back to home culture didn't take long. A cozy cottage within fifty paces of a murmuring stream welcomed us to our new neighborhood. A large picture window overlooked the stream, and rows and rows of daffodils lined the fence. Wanda was right—the house was perfect. And a surprise came with the house: a black-and-white border collie that had been left behind by the previous renters, who were also in the military. Cuddles turned out to be an incredible watchdog and companion for the children. I never feared their wandering very far or falling into the creek. Cuddles would nudge them back.

Of course the creek became our favorite place to play. Lori helped me pile up rocks to form a wading pool. Holding baby Ernie's arms, we walked in the flow of the stream, but mostly he would sit and splash in the water, trying his best to help big sister catch little fish. Right off, Ernie showed an interest in the creepy-crawly things of earth—frogs, toads, and snakes—while Lori chased butterflies and picked wildflowers.

Ernie, naturally talented in finding ways to entertain himself, provided for never a dull moment. Like when he was five months old, he would pull himself up onto the sofa and then roll off it and over the floor. Lori shrieked, "Unie, *no—no!* You get boo-boo! *No—no!*" Over and over my little bundle of mischief would roll and laugh. Such fun to tease big sister!

Surrounded by giant oaks and falling leaves, one fall day Lori and I took on the task of raking leaves while at the same time Ernie played in a big pile of leaves. That afternoon when Lori's four-year-old cousin Lisa arrived, she asked, "Lori, what did you do today?"

In a two-year-old version of l's and r's, Lori replied, "Unie pway in weaves all day—Wowie wake weaves all day wong—Powh Wowie!"

Wanda and Lisa began to giggle. "Powh Wowie," they chuckled

simultaneously. *Powh Wowie* stuck. Even to this day it's part of family entertainment to say, "Powh Wowie, what did you do today?"

Nothing in my life had ever been more satisfying than being a mother: feeding my babies; bathing them; teaching them how to tie their shoes; riding them on a bicycle; helping them feed the dog; helping them brush their teeth; playing with them; sharing them with the grandmas, aunts, uncles, and cousins; and listening to their chatter—but best of all, the snuggling and love. I felt pride for every little thing they did, marveling at how quickly they learned songs about Jesus that I had learned as a child.

That entire year, the sunshine of God's love shone on my babies and in my heart, with the exception of one thing. It was hard for me to wrap my mind around the idea of the monster war going on. When I watched the news, I feared for Eric being in war territory. *Will he come back alive?* I was surrounded by loved ones living in a free country—but he was not. The contrast was surreal. He was caught up in a long brutal war that never seemed to end. I'd heard terrible stories about the horrors faced by servicemen during wartime. *What stories will he tell when he gets back? What will he be like?*

Eric's letters were few and far between. "Everything is top secret, not much I can write about. Our ship drops anchor every ten to fifteen days to receive mail. Pictures of you and the kids boost my morale—keep them coming!" The year he was gone was longer than the time we had lived together stateside as a family. I wondered if there would ever come a time when we could get to know each other better. I hoped for better times.

Eric's arrival home

In March the following year, a long-anticipated letter from Eric announced his return to the base in San Diego.

> Don't worry about meeting the ship. I've put in for a two-week leave and I'll be flying to Sacramento. Pick me up at the airport. Bring the kids—can't wait to see you. After my leave, I'll be flying back to San Diego where I'll be stationed for several months. I want you and the kids to move to navy housing there. I've reserved a two-bedroom apartment and have arranged for a moving van to

pick up our belongings and get you moved. It's the best and most affordable place for us right now. You'll be near the commissary and all its perks, and you'll have plenty of navy-wife company. At least for a few months, before I'm deployed again, we can be a family.

The housing complex consisted of rows and rows of units with four apartments in each unit. Living there was like living in a dormitory: always someone to talk to. Carmen, a pleasant lady living next door, was from Trinidad. She helped me learn Trinidad Spanish, and I helped her with her English. Kathy, who also lived in our unit, was from Tennessee. Being a veteran navy wife of many years, she knew the answers to everything. Soon I bonded with her and her four children. We formed a support team for several of the younger wives. I could identify with some of the stories I heard about how the war had changed their husbands' behavior. We shared a common realization: *anticipation of a possible blowup often creates a distance in relationships*. One woman described it in a nutshell: *kind of like walking on eggshells*. Some of the wives talked about how they had heard their husbands brag about cheating on their wives, or how they came back addicted to alcohol or drugs. Occasionally there would be a wife-beating. I remember one in particular, a young girl only eighteen years old. Her husband returned, not wanting to be married anymore: "First he loves me, and then he doesn't. He swings back and forth. He has asked for a divorce. I don't know what to do." Exhausted, she returned to her home state to live near her mother.

We hadn't been in navy housing long when I noticed that my husband was not the easygoing man I had married. He was moody and edgy most of the time. Before, he had occasionally relaxed with a beer; now a can would always be in his hand. "Be glad it's not whiskey. Last summer, due to problems with the air conditioning units, our ship ended up having an extended stay in Subic Bay for repair. We sailors, on weekends, would go into Olongapo to 'bar hop,' and for entertainment."

"Entertainment? What kind?"

"You wouldn't want to know. Before you get judgmental on me, just remember, while you had the comforts of home, I didn't. The heat was intolerable. In port, our crew would sleep on mattresses topside of the ship. You don't know what heat is like until you live in a monsoon climate without air conditioning! It helped to go into town and cool off.

War Comes Home

Drinking calms me down; don't worry about it."

I remember the first time I was awakened by Eric yelling out in his sleep. Suddenly he was back in the war zone. When I tried to reach out to him, he snarled, "Get away from me!"

"Eric, I want to help. Can you talk about it?"

"*No!* Complaints in the service are viewed as signs of weakness. Do yourself—*and me*—a favor and don't ask about the war again!" I was in total disbelief. *Who is this man?* Eric stayed true to his word: he would not talk about his active war duty.

What, I wondered, could have produced such a total change in a person in such a short time? I tried to imagine the things he might have experienced. Had he been badly frightened, over and over? That seemed likely. Had he witnessed horrific things being done to women and children? Another dreadful possibility. I remembered friends of my dad, World War II veterans, swapping stories about their ghastly wartime experiences. I shuddered to think about what Eric might have been through in the past months and what he was going through still.

It helped me to gain some idea about what could be causing his behavior. The more urgent question was how I should relate to him as the man he was now. He was in his own dark world; nothing I said or did made any difference. I was still weighing my choices when he was again deployed to Vietnam. Relieved for the time being, I settled back into the world of my children and my friends. Twice more he was deployed, and twice he came back, surlier and moodier than ever.

Much later, when PTSD had become a diagnosis, I became more aware of the kinds of issues that plagued the combat troops. Eventually, I came to better understand my husband's behavior. In addition to the normal horrors of war, unbelievable atrocities were inflicted on the civilian population by the Vietcong. Death lay in the streets. The servicemen carried the visual torture in their subconscious, and PTSD resulted. In addition, the Vietnam War was so controversial that returning vets were vilified, with epithets such as "baby-killer" hurled at them. It is no wonder that so many veterans of various wars have had to struggle to readjust to civilian life. Even today some still suffer the aftereffects.

Eric most certainly did; in so many ways, he was an enigma. Would our relationship survive the stress of his wartime choices and his damaged personality? Time alone would tell.

CHAPTER 24

The Light Shines in the Darkness

After Eric returned, the commotion that had already begun in our relationship lasted through the summer. Just before the ship was to pull out again, a situation of epic proportions flared up. (I will spare the painful details.) Since I wouldn't comply with an ultimatum he laid down, Eric stipulated that our marriage take a recess and I not write to him while he was gone. As far as he was concerned the marriage was over. I felt sorrowful, angry, and relieved at the same time. Our situation seemed hopeless. Thereupon we agreed to move forward with divorce when he returned.

Six months later I received a letter requesting that I meet the ship on its return to the naval base. Hundreds of sailors waved from the ship as it pulled into harbor. I stood in the waiting crowd, not knowing what to expect, unease gnawing at my throat. Then I spotted him, walking down the plank with a big dimpled smile and standing taller than most of the other sailors. In his arms he carried gifts he had acquired in the Philippines.

We resumed life together, and our relationship did seem to improve for a while. But as time went on we drifted apart, becoming even more alienated. Then an unexpected reality made its appearance: I was pregnant—clearly, not a good time to consider a breakup. We agreed, for the present at least, to try to make our marriage work.

As the pregnancy progressed, Eric was not tolerant of my limitations, and neither was I. Of course, God was always there, never harshly judgmental, always tolerant of my humanness. If only I could have stayed close enough to Him to be aware of His acceptance! But in my misery, I had cut myself off from God emotionally, and I figured I could handle life on my own.

When you pick a flower, it begins to wilt, because it has lost its connection with the living plant. When we lose connection with Jesus, we begin to wilt. Hence, on days when everything seemed to go wrong, I found myself to be harshly judgmental and unforgiving of myself. I thought, *Surely God can't love me. I'm just not good enough.*

Yet through this difficult time, the love of my children and my love for the baby growing inside kept me going. I did the best I could to put on a cheerful face and keep their lives happy, singing songs from my childhood, such as "Jesus Wants Me for a Sunbeam," and telling them over and over how much God loved them.

Although mostly on duty, Eric was home-based the entire time of my pregnancy. A few days before he was to be deployed again, I went into labor. Two weeks shy of full term, I arrived at the hospital with strong contractions. I was still there two days later, laboring hard, drained by the pain, and desperate with exhaustion. I knew that if a baby is not born after twenty hours of contractions, the labor is considered to be prolonged and possibly abnormal. By now I was frightened. What was going on? Why couldn't I seem to have this baby? How might the prolonged labor be affecting my unborn child? And what would become of me if I couldn't deliver it soon? I couldn't relax. The labor was going nowhere, and the fact that I was so tied up in knots made it even worse. I was frantic with fear for my baby and for myself.

Lying there fearful, helpless, and exhausted, I found myself reliving past mistakes and failures. Satan whispered, *God doesn't love you—you're not good enough—you are a failure.* Worn out, not only by the prolonged labor, but also by years of trying to build a marriage against all odds while shielding my children from the conflict, I was a sitting duck for the onslaught of false charges Satan began lobbing at me. *You're no good. You're a failure—always have been, always will be. How could God love someone like you?* I was swept into a tsunami of despair as he continued. *Why not just end it here and now?*

Irrational in my exhaustion, I began to think, *If I'm gone, the doctors can still save the baby, and Mama and Wanda can raise it. I'm too much of a mess to be a good mom anymore.* Finally I took action. I carefully removed a razor blade from the razor in my overnight case, and when the nurses were elsewhere, I slid off the bed and made my way to the bathroom. But before I had a chance to follow through with my intent, God came to my rescue by sending Nurse Eleanor as His ambassador. She took in the scene at a glance and began to pray. Both of us were in tears as she gently guided me back to the bed.

Then the Spirit of God moved in. To prove His love, my baby daughter was born with no pain—a miracle birth with no pain or even discomfort. Tenderly, He spoke to my heart: *"Marlyn, my precious daughter, I love you. You are Mine."* Euphorically enfolded in God's tender love, I wasn't afraid anymore. The lesson was obvious: The enemy of my soul had attacked me severely. Alone, I couldn't win this battle. With Jesus, I couldn't lose. In my brokenness, I was saved by the supernatural power and love of God. Here, twenty-five years old and at the lowest point of my life, I began to learn who God really is. This marked the beginning of a process of deliverance from strongholds that had been beyond my control. Clearly, I began to see the common thread throughout all my life: "Jesus loves me; this I know." Like a surgeon, He skillfully put me back together, no longer to doubt His love.

From the moment the nurse placed baby Tamara in my arms, she snuggled into my heart. God had created another masterpiece. *"I will give this little one a comforting and tender heart. She will go through times of hardship, but she will learn to live above the thorns. She will bless many."* God dances and sings when babies are born,

> For the Lord your God is living among you.
> He is a mighty savior.
> He will take delight in you with gladness.
> With his love, he will calm all your fears.
> He will rejoice over you with joyful songs (Zephaniah 3:17, NLT).

Broken windows, open doors

Faith often enters through the back doors of broken windows and shattered dreams. Our family appeared to be beautifully wrapped, but on the inside it was shattered. When Eric finished his second enlistment in the navy, his father came for a visit. He lived in Atlanta and convinced us that a move there would be good for our family, where we could recover from the stresses of the war. *God, I'm tired of brokenness—is this an open door?* Moving to Atlanta would mean tearful goodbyes to loved ones and friends and uncertainty as to what lay ahead. I wondered: *Will I ever have a place to call home?* But the adventurer in me decided it was worth a try.

Eric's excellent work record landed him employment with Southern Railroad at a good salary. He started as a conductor and then trained to be an engineer. His regular run was to Greenville, South Carolina. He was gone over half the time, but when he was home, we made an effort to keep the marriage alive. But wherever you go, there you are, and vestiges of Vietnam remained. Eric was in need of recovery from combat PTSD—it had adversely affected both of us, but therapy was not available. I thought that the influence of his father and stepmother would certainly help, and for a while it did.

I longed for a deeper relationship and a closer walk with Jesus. I joined the Belvedere Seventh-day Adventist Church, a church alive to the truth of God's Word and the power of Holy Spirit–led worship, prayer, and teaching. There were many children in the church, and I became actively involved in the children's divisions, first as a teacher in Cradle Roll, then as the Kindergarten division leader, a position I enjoyed and held for many years. Jubilant in the friendship of many beautiful Christians, my heart was overjoyed. How good it was to be in a community of believers! How wonderful it was to have my children enrolled in a Christian school! The children and I had many friends. How I longed to share this with Eric! I invited him to attend church with the children and me, hoping that would fix things. He did join us for a while, but although he was physically present, his heart was not in it. He had a mind-set of his own, with no intention of joining my world. Inevitably, our marriage collapsed.

My story is not too different from that of many others who are spiritually single. An anonymous person once described it this way: "Being married to an unchurched spouse is a lonely road on which one frequently feels isolated. It's akin to residing in a different dimension from one's mate; the inability to share spiritual insights and truths is painful, and the thing you hold dearest in life cannot be comprehended by the person you love. You are spiritually single. It often is heartbreaking and frustrating."

The alcoholism started all over again. When he was drunk and angry, I would pack the children into the car and take them on an outing to Stone Mountain. We called it our home away from home. One day in an out-of-control uproar, the dam broke, and Eric insisted on divorce. His rationalization was, "I don't want to be married anymore. I want to live my own life. I didn't grow up with the morals you grew up with. Besides, I can't be faithful to one woman, and I don't see the wrong in it. I have a girlfriend in Greenville, and she's not the first. I know what your church teaches. You have grounds for divorce."

As I look back, I think Eric knew he was losing the ability to control his angry outbursts. He insisted that I keep the house and the new car we had bought, making it clear that he would move into an apartment. I have come to believe that he loved me and the children enough to let us go. He was afraid for us and didn't like subjecting us to his outbursts of temper. I finally recognized how detrimental his disease was to my own health and safety. When the abuse had crossed the line and escalated to the danger point, I called his dad, who helped me file for divorce. Our nine-year marriage was over in thirty days.

Divorce can be more emotionally fraught than losing a loved one. When a loved one dies, there's closure. With divorce, you don't get closure ever—especially when there are children involved. In my case it meant leaving my part-time job at Home Health Education Service to begin working full time as a receptionist at the nearby conference headquarters of our church denomination. It also meant a battle with ever-increasing depression.

When Mama called asking if Lori and Tamara could fly out for a month, I agreed to let them go. Ernie didn't want to go. He wanted to stay with me. His best friend, Butch, lived nearby. Butch's mother provided childcare for Ernie while I worked and invited him to go on a camping trip and outings.

With my girls gone and Ernie on a camping trip, I was alone for the weekend. Being alone flattened my self-confidence and focus. I prayed to be spared another day of guilt and depression. I didn't want to live a life of sorrow, and I didn't know how to stop it. As my emotions spiraled downward, I lay in a sweat, praying that the Lord would deliver me from the nightmare my life had become. I cried out, "God, can't You make me just a little less broken?"

God answered my prayer by allowing even more brokenness, and a spirit of fear came over me as if I'd been physically fighting a vastly superior entity. Terror gripped me. I'd been alone for so long—alone with the fears and emotions I had worked so hard to hide. Satan, the enemy, waged ever-fiercer warfare against me. This demon seemed unbeatable; I couldn't knock him out. But just when I felt like giving up, I decided to pray all night. I fell asleep praying. As I was sleeping, I had a vision of Jesus. He smiled at me with an expression of benevolence and majesty that could belong to no one but the King of the heavenly court. In the words of one Christian writer who had a similar experience,

> I knew at once that He was acquainted with every circumstance of my life and all my inner thoughts and feelings.
> ... Laying His hand upon my head, [He] said: "Fear not." The sound of His sweet voice thrilled my heart with a happiness it had never before experienced.[1]

Escaping the devil's stronghold is a humbling experience. Instead of trying to figure everything out, I simply asked for help. I got better for one reason: I surrendered to God. In the future, in times of difficulty, I would remember the loving eyes of Jesus, and the beauty and simplicity of trusting in Him would dawn upon my soul. My heart would fill with strength.

In spite of my difficult situation, I still had to be functional for work and for my children. With God's help I managed to pick myself up and dust myself off. I had at the core of my being a steely resolve to do right by myself and my children. God was fixing the broken pieces in my life. He was preparing me for everything I had prayed for. The inner fire was burning bright. *He* was my Spouse, and I could trust Him.

So what now? Where should I go from here? I didn't know. But I looked forward to the journey. I wanted to turn the page, sell the house, and start a new chapter in my life, but I really had no idea where to start. One thing I knew for certain was that I would include God in my journey. The answer came when the denominational conference for which I worked moved its headquarters to Calhoun, Georgia. I sold the house and moved with them.

God led me into a life of faith and recovery for a purpose. I may not know how to adequately express *how* I got from there to where I am today, but every day I get a better understanding of *why*.

The Light Shines in the Darkness

"God's Word is not a self-help book on successful living. It is God Himself coming to me with His presence, His mind, His heart; it is God Himself strengthening me from the inside out, building my core. In His Word He meets me, changes me, and provides for me."[2]

---

1. Ellen G. White, *Early Writings* (Hagerstown, MD: Review and Herald®, 2000), 80.
2. Kathie Lichtenwalter.

CHAPTER 25

When God Writes Your Love Story

Ernie swiped a second helping of scalloped potatoes. "Hey, Mom, Loren's sweet on you. I can tell. Why don't you propose to him?" Placing a piece of buttered cornbread on my young son's plate, I smiled as he licked his lips.

"That topsy-turvy nature walk he planned was a blast, and he plays ball with me." Ernie gulped down a bite. "And I like that he knows a lot about snakes and lizards and such. I dig him, Mom—he's cool. Why don't you propose to him?"

Amused by my nine-year-old's sudden overture, I played along. "I hardly think that would happen, son. I'm glad you like him. But you know it's the man's job to propose."

"Well, if that's the case, I'm going to pray that he will . . ."

Tamara glanced at her brother and then at me. "Mommy, I like that Pastor Loren's a preacher and that he loves Jesus." Her cheeks flushed bright with excitement. "How cool it would be to have a preacher for a daddy!"

"Why do you think that, Tamara?"

"He could baptize me. Imagine that, my very own daddy baptizing me." My seven-year-old giggled. Ever since her brother had been baptized, this was foremost in her mind.

I glanced at Lori. She fought to keep a smile from her face as she scooped food into her mouth. "I've got homework to do, Mama, and it's my turn to do dishes." She jumped to her feet and began clearing the table.

I gazed out the kitchen window at the golden sliver of light brightening the gray in the clouds. It spoke volumes to my heart. *Was this the harbinger of a dramatic turn of events?*

My mind traveled back to how it had begun on a nippy October afternoon. No sooner had I sat down at my receptionist desk after lunch when the door opened, and the conference evangelist came striding purposefully through the lobby.

"Hi, Marlyn! You and the kids are invited to our house for dinner tonight! Plan to arrive around six."

At that moment a tall young gentleman pulled into the parking lot. He intended to get to the conference office ahead of Pastor Jim Hiner and look the receptionist over. Then he could decide whether to meet her or not.

"Hi, Loren," Pastor Jim enthusiastically called out. "Let me introduce you to Marlyn. She's our dinner guest tonight. Of course, you'll be there too." In his usual decisive manner, Pastor Jim considered it to be all arranged and quickly wrote out the directions to his house.

Having never met Loren, at first I didn't realize he was a pastor and only later heard what the backstory was. It seems the local conference headquarters had sent two evangelists, Jim Hiner and Howard Boling, to help build up one of the three churches Loren pastored. The denomination strongly encourages its pastors to have wives, so when they discovered his single status, they determined to make it a priority to get him married. At the conclusion of the series of evangelistic meetings, Howard had a sudden inspiration. "Loren, I know who you should meet," he declared.

"Who?" he asked.

"Marlyn—the receptionist at the conference office."

"Of course, Howard, why didn't I think of that?" Pastor Jim turned to Loren. "I became acquainted with Marlyn when I held evangelistic meetings in Atlanta. She was my greeter and organized the paperwork. Her assistance was invaluable! By all means, I give you the green light!"

"OK, what's she like?" Loren cautiously inquired.

Howard pondered briefly. "I would describe her as queenly. Yes, queenly."

What Howard didn't know was that Loren's kid brother, Steve, had been composing whimsical Ogden Nash-style poetry documenting Loren's encounters with a few girls he had dated during the preceding year. It was obvious to Steve he was in pursuit of a wife. Euphemistically he had labeled them "Queen of the South," "Queen of the North," and "Queen of the East," depending on their geographic location. So when

When God Writes Your Love Story

Howard used the word *queenly*, Loren was immediately intrigued. Would "Queen of the West" be the title of his brother's next poem?

Late afternoon sunlight drifted through the dining room window as Mrs. Hiner dished out a delectable fresh-from-the-garden meal, completed by a basket of sliced homemade bread and apple pie for dessert.

After dinner, Pastor Jim whispered, "Let's sneak outside, kids, and give Mom and Pastor Loren a chance to get acquainted." He guided them along as they snuck out the back door.

Making his way back inside, Pastor Jim took a seat next to his wife in their large living room. After a short flow of conversation, he stated, "Velda and I need to catch up with our reading while you two get acquainted. Pay no attention to us."

Hoisting magazines to cover their faces, Jim and Velda occasionally peered up as they pretended to read.

Loren lived four hours away and didn't have time to waste. If this new acquaintance was to be the "Queen of Queens," he must find out as much as he could. It was intriguing to find out we were both half-Norwegian, that we were California transplants, and that the bulk of our relatives lived in the Northwest. At the opportune time, Loren snuggled in a little closer and began to ask a barrage of questions. Ultimately he popped a question he deemed of utmost significance—"Do you read your Bible much?"

"I just finished Isaiah and I'm reading Jeremiah—interesting prelude leading up to the Gospels. The Gospels are my favorite, especially the book of John."

"Whoa, when do you find time, what with you working full time and raising three kids?"

"The kids know their mama needs quiet time with Jesus. I drive them to a nature spot, and they play while I read my Bible. Before long I join them in the creek, a hike, or whatever they want to do. They know they'll get a reward if they are good, and that Mama will be a better Mama when she reads her Bible."

Loren quizzed me about what I had read, and then he asked another important question—"Do you like to cook?"

"I don't follow recipes much; cooking's a natural thing. Yes, I do love to cook."

"Do you ever make homemade bread?"

Beyond Ashes

"Funny you should ask. I started baking bread two weeks ago. Stop by sometime and I'll give you a loaf."

Loren's perspective: *She cooks! She bakes! She sews! She reads! She's spiritually strong! She's attractive! She's intelligent! Hmm, a Proverbs 31 woman—at last I've found her! Forward march with the courtship!*

My perspective: *I've never met a man so interested in finding out what I'm like. But, good heavens, by the questions he's asking, I'd say he's in search of a wife!*

In a short time Loren's kid brother began writing "Queen of the West"—a whimsical poem beginning with "Hiner's Honey is Finer..."

More than a fairy tale

As a kid growing up, my favorite fairy tale was Cinderella. I dreamed of finding my Prince Charming: a perfect love that would last my entire life. But somewhere in the midst of the cycle of temporary romances, my dreams had splintered.

Though I found Pastor Jim's enthusiasm intriguing, being a pastor's wife wasn't exactly at the top of my dream list. I was well aware that marriage to a pastor in our conference could mean moving every five to eight years. I had just bought a new house; my car was paid for; I enjoyed my work at the conference; the children were in a church school that could school them through twelfth grade. For the first time in a long time, I felt comfortably settled for the long haul. Remarriage was not on my mind.

Reflecting on the relationship as it developed, I grew more and more apprehensive. *Wasn't it Daddy's dream that I get involved in mission service, preferably as a missionary nurse, which he later altered to a missionary teacher?* He had even prayed about it. Back then my ambition had been (and still was) to graduate from college, make a good salary, and settle down in style. *Marriage again? Not for a long time! But what does God have in mind? Certainly Daddy would've approved my marrying a pastor. Is God answering Daddy's prayer?* I puzzled over that thought. Daddy had had more prayers answered than anyone else I knew. Certainly he had a direct connection with God! And yet...

Ernie's surprising pitch about a marriage proposal had taken place on a Sunday evening after Loren had visited us that weekend. A week later, when the kids and I were getting ready for church, Ernie's face was enlightened with boyish eagerness. "Mom, Loren is going to propose to you today."

"Yes, dear." I smiled indulgently. "We'll see."

"He will! I've been praying and I dreamed about it last night! It's going to happen, Mom! Loren will propose to you *today*!" Confidence rang in his voice. I was amused at his certainty. This was the day Loren planned to come, but a proposal? I considered it highly unlikely and dismissed the thought. *Haven't Loren and I discussed the idea that a courtship should last at least two years?*

Autumn's frosty breath chilled the air as Loren arrived to a fresh-cooked meal, the aroma, I hoped, tantalizing to his nostrils as he walked in the door. The children had been invited by neighbors for an evening of food and games at the academy. For the first time since we had met, Loren and I enjoyed a quiet romantic evening meal with candles and soft music. When the kids returned, Tamara announced, "It's time for worship," and Loren read them a story. We knelt for prayer, and soon they were tucked away in bed.

As we sat together on the sofa talking, Loren whipped out a beautiful card with a red rose in the front. Inside was a poem handwritten in German. He read it in fluent German.

"Dû bist mîn, ich bin dîn: des solt dû gewis sîn. Dû bist beslozzen in mînem herzen: verlorn ist das sluzzelîn: dû muost ouch immêr darinne sîn."

A note was written at the bottom: "I know you like poetry, so I thought I'd let you try your hand at this. If you run into a dead end, you may have to ask me for a translation. I might give it to you."

"Yes please, a translation."

Taking my hands in his, he looked into my eyes, "You are mine, I am yours; of this you may be certain. You are locked in my heart. The little key is lost, so you must stay inside forever."

Recalling Ernie's forecast that morning, and our conversation before the poem, I was certain Loren was working up to a proposal—a quick glance at the clock—one minute before midnight. *He's taking his time—Ernie was sure he would propose today. I don't want my son's faith to be crushed. I don't want his heart to be broken.*

"If you don't propose soon, it will be tomorrow and not today," the words tumbled out.

Beyond Ashes

"Marlyn, will you marry me?"

"Yes, yes," I responded—exactly five seconds before the clock struck the midnight hour. Deeply moved by what had just taken place, I told Loren for the first time about Ernie's prayer and dream. We were blown away by how providentially God had answered a little boy's prayer, and how quickly it had happened.

A wide-open door
The next morning I woke up jittery: *I've known Loren only two months—how can I marry someone I hardly know?* Appealing to an Authority higher than myself, I cried out, "Lord, if this indeed is Your will, open the door wide. If it's not Your will, *please* close the door."

Two days I prayed. Two days I pondered the situation, seeking direction not only from God but from the conference president, the secretary, and the treasurer. Each fully approved, offering a prayer of blessing. Pastor Harold Metcalf, my mentor at the job where I had previously worked—a father figure to everyone—encouraged, "I believe you have the makings of a wonderful pastor's wife. I couldn't be more pleased."

Hmm, I must seek the approval of the three most important people on my planet.

Lori, who was twelve going on eighteen, took pleasure in big sisterhood. "Since you're asking my opinion, that brother of mine's been *trouble* lately and needs a dad's firm hand, and Mama—" She paused. "If marrying Loren is what you want, it's OK by me."

Tamara stood nearby. "I can hardly wait for the wedding! Hey, where's Ernie?"

"Turning cartwheels!" laughed Ernie. "I'm the one that flipped the switch, remember?"

When I called Mama, she got excited and began to cry! "*Mi Boquita Linda,* I'm so happy for you, and how happy your daddy would be. God has given you another chance for happiness just like He has given me. You can be sure Ephraim [my new stepdad] and I will come to the wedding!" Mama's approval was the affirmation that quieted my reservations.

I had asked God to open the door or close the door. God didn't just give me a gentle nudge; He said, "Trust Me," and shoved me through. Two days after the proposal, I gave the Great Lover, God, the pen to author my love story. I was willing to marry the man He chose for me. Peace flooded my soul.

Loren's reality was less complicated. One of the church members had penned a letter to President Cummings, stating that it was important to the church that they have a pastor with a wife and children. Deeming it indeed important, the president urged him to find a wife.

"I've found the girl I've been praying for, and I'll be providing you with a ready-made family. You will love them as much as I do." Cheering and clapping rose from the congregation when Loren detailed our engagement. Their prayers had been answered! They would have a pastor with a wife and children!

A family for Christmas!
Bartering for time didn't work. Pastor Jim, who would be the officiating minister, proclaimed, "We'll give the churches a family for Christmas," and he set the date for Saturday, December 20, giving us two weeks to plan the wedding.

A friend volunteered to make my wedding dress. "No time for a fancy dress," she said as we picked an simple but elegant pattern. I made Lori's and Tamara's dresses.

The days leading up to the wedding passed quickly. Parishioners went all out to provide a beautiful Christmas wedding. The church looked the way I had always imagined a wedding to be: red poinsettias brightened the entrance; ribbons, lace, and mistletoe adorned the pews; a heart-shaped candelabra was centered on the rostrum; candlesticks and ornate pillars topped with white poinsettia plants accentuated each side of the candelabra. Soft organ music and vocal musical selections added to the solemn beauty of the event.

The wedding party was indeed a family event: Lori looked like a princess as she floated down the aisle serving as my maid of honor; Tamara fairly danced as she carried the flower girl basket, carefully dropping red and pink rose petals; and Ernie glowed as he escorted me down the aisle. When the minister said, "Who gives this woman to this man?" Ernie grandly declared, "My sisters and I do," and led me to the man he had prayed to be his daddy.

Weddings are made for happy tears. There wasn't a dry eye as Loren sang his vows and Wilma Boling sang my vows.

Beyond Ashes

Loren's vows:

> Walk hand in hand with me through all eternity
> Have faith, believe in me, give me your hand
> Love is a symphony of perfect harmony
> When lovers such as we walk hand in hand
> Be not afraid, for I am with you all the while
> So lift your head up high and look toward the sky
> Walk hand in hand with me, this is our destiny
> No greater love could be, walk hand in hand
> Walk with me.

My vows:

> Thy people will be my people my love
> Whither thou goest, I will go.
> Wherever thou lodgest, I will lodge.
> Thy people will be my people my love,
> Whither thou goest, I will go!
> For as in that story, long ago,
> The same sweet love story, now is so,
> Thy people shall be my people my love,
> Whither thou goest, I will go!
> Wherever thou lodgest, I will lodge.

Pastor Hiner pronounced us husband and wife, and Howard Boling sealed the love story in the heavenly courts as he sang "The Lord's Prayer."

Our wedding was indeed a breathtaking taste of heaven on earth, a joyful celebration of a family brought together by the providence of God in answer to a little boy's prayer.

So proceeds the beauty of a God-written love story—a story of togetherness through life's storms, of sacrificial, selfless, lasting, unconditional love—a story of love in action: the kind that lasts a lifetime.

EPILOGUE

He Restores My Soul

God rescues and heals.

Time and time again throughout my life, God has rescued me from peril and endangerment.

As a three-year-old toddling away from the safety of my grandmother's presence, I knocked on the one door in the entire village where those within drugged me and would have sold me into slavery. But when those who loved me prayed, God disrupted Satan's plan and miraculously delivered me, bringing joy to the hearts of friends and family and glory to His name.

Twenty years later, as a naïve, trusting young woman, I inadvertently wandered into Satan's territory. Once again, the plans of a man who drugged me and who would have stolen and sold me or maybe killed me were foiled, this time by two strong young men who, enabled by God, saw just in time what was happening and rescued me.

When God rescues us, the marvelous thing is that He takes the evil Satan has planned for us and makes the outcome even better than it would have been had the enemy never launched his nefarious plans. As in the stories I've shared with you, God has rescued me over and over again, turning Satan's machinations to His glory!

Equally important, God has healed me.

Christianity teaches that restoration involves embracing oneself as a child of God, faults and all—turning our faults and flaws over to the Creator God for restoration, and trusting that He will miraculously remove them. In our human nature, when we've been deeply wounded, trusting in God's grace and mercy is not easy to do, for the pain is cemented deep within the soul.

Being of a sensitive nature, I found myself harshly judgmental and unforgiving of myself for the times I had failed. I wanted to help others,

Beyond Ashes

but I felt useless. "Help" and "Thanks" were my basic prayers, but sometimes I felt awkward and out of place to go beyond that. A disapproving voice inside my head said, *I'm not good enough for this. I'll wait until I've cleaned up my act.*

Fortunately, God does not think we are useless. He knows us inside and out. He knows our limits. He does not pity us as poor and pathetic: His compassion is tender, encouraging, and loving. Rich in love, God makes everything come out all right, and He puts victims back on their feet. When I make mistakes, it's better than all right, because it's my failures more than my achievements that open me up to His redeeming grace. My turning to Him is simply done out of love and need for my Savior.

As a pastor's wife, I struggled to comprehend and deal with the harsh realities of the world. I met many bruised and hurt lives, and I had hurts of my own. My heart was knit with compassion, but I felt at a loss to know how to help. I had long felt emotional healing to be a vital part of God's plan for restoration, but how could I help other wounded souls when I was still struggling with my own pain?

God knew what I needed and provided the resources at just the right time. A desire for personal growth, as well as for helping others, led me to attain accreditation in Christian counseling. Part of the classwork involved significant *hands-on training* in processing losses and grievances through group therapy. I learned that before helping others, I must first learn to help myself. When one is retracing one's steps through old traumas, the goal is restoration that will bring peace of mind, resulting in joyful living. As part of my recovery, I was encouraged to write a goodbye letter to my little brother, Milton, and read it to the group. Crying open tears and receiving emotional support was indeed healing, and it helped me to bring closure to his untimely death.

The Bible-based coursework not only educated my mind but also helped me develop a closer, more intimate fellowship with Jesus. Thus God prepared me for a spiritual and emotional awakening of heart, mind, and soul, that I might better share His love. This training was helpful in the many roles I filled as a wife, mother, pastor's wife, children and youth ministries leader, and later, jail ministry—and now in the writing of this book. In these roles, I've repeatedly found that the pain I've suffered has enabled me to empathize with others needing healing:

rape victims, grieving souls, battered wives, struggling single moms, and others besieged with diverse kinds of suffering—physical, emotional, and spiritual. Suffering borne with grace bestows a kind of wisdom that cannot be attained by any other means. I realize that part of my suffering has been bestowed by the enemy and part by my own choices, but God has supplied the grace to bear all of it.

A final ingredient in the healing had to come from my own heart. An unforgiving spirit was an abscess within my soul. God prepared my heart to forgive, but before I could do that, I had to learn how much God loved me. When someone betrays my trust, humanly speaking I have the right not to forgive. I have come to embrace the idea that forgiving is not about feeling; it's about obeying and honoring Jesus, who died on the cross to save sinners. Myself a sinner, Jesus gives me the gift of His forgiveness. Who am I not to forgive, when Jesus has forgiven me? When I receive forgiveness, it's like receiving refreshment to my soul, like taking a drink of living water. When I give forgiveness to someone who hurts me, it works the same way. I may cry over the hurt, but it's OK, because my life is right with Jesus, and He gives me peace.

As an addendum to the stories I've shared in this book, I will list three major cases of forgiveness that have brought refreshment to my soul.

Sometimes something has happened in our life that is so devastating we hang on to it. Such was the case of the stern-faced dean of students who had ousted me from college. I still carried the image of his cruel face glaring at me. I had to learn how to erase the image of a pitiless man's face in order to see God's face smiling on me. A golden surprise was in the making: I do not believe it was accidental that while shopping one day, I happened to cross paths with George Akers, the beloved dean of students during my freshman college year. He had recently moved into the area where I was living. I spontaneously approached him, startled at the ease with which I shared the story about the ousting and how badly it had hurt me. With tears in his eyes, Dean Akers held my hands and said, "Marlyn, I'm so sorry this happened to you. I can tell it still hurts your heart. Would it help if I apologized on his behalf?" I nodded a tearful yes. Dean Akers, in the middle of the store with people all around, offered a prayer for me and a prayer of forgiveness for the man who had hurt me. A warm sensation of peace washed over my heart. His gracious gift of kindness melted me into compassion for the man whose stern face I had

Beyond Ashes

not yet forgotten. I do not know what became of his hardened heart, but I do know that he was covered with prayer, and I hope to meet him again in the earth made new.

Once I made the decision to forgive Silas, there was peace in my heart, because I knew that's what God wanted me to do. I simply asked God to deliver and restore Silas to His grace. It must've worked. Years later, when Lori was twenty-one, I learned from Mama that Silas was living near where she lived and that he had married a single lady with a young child and had adopted the child as his own. He and his wife also had a child of their own. Lori chose to meet her biological father. While visiting Mama in California, it was arranged that Loren, Lori, and I meet with Silas and his wife at a restaurant. In this meeting, I witnessed the grace of God at work—Silas had indeed turned his life around. He accepted Lori as his daughter, and she in future years enjoyed getting acquainted with him and her new family. The apology I had not received early on was offered profusely. He praised me for the courage I had shown and the fine daughter I had raised. He was kind to Loren and thanked him for filling the role of father to Lori on his behalf, as he had likewise done with his wife's daughter. This indeed was a reward for choosing the way of forgiveness. Years later, when Silas was dying of cancer, his wife called, asking that I pray for him. Lori flew to California to be with her father before he went to his rest. He passed with peace in his heart, the peace of knowing he had made things right with his Maker, with his daughter, and with his fellow man.

A few years ago I received a call from Ernie. It warmed my heart to learn that his father, Eric, had enrolled in a treatment center for alcoholism and had successfully conquered the addiction. Later, Ernie called again to let me know his father was dying of esophageal cancer. I had forgiven Eric and had been praying for him all along. Now I prayed more earnestly that he receive spiritual healing. I talked with Eric on the phone, and he apologized for the trauma he had brought upon me and others in the family. Ernie spent quality time with his dad before he died. When the doctor gave him just a short time to live, Tamara visited her dad in his home. During this time, his pain temporarily subsided, and they were able to talk for several hours. His struggle was with not feeling forgiven, not sensing a connection with God. After Tamara left, his wife witnessed him on his knees, agonizing in prayer. She offered to help him but he refused, saying, "I have to do this myself. It's between me and God," and he remained on his knees a long time. Tamara and her husband prayed intercessory prayer that he would not suffer long and that he would die in peace. God answered that prayer. Although the doctor had given him two weeks to live, Eric went to his rest the day they prayed. His wife witnessed a peace in his face she had never seen before. He passed away with a cleansed heart.

* * * * *

There's a peaceful park-like cemetery in the Northern California foothills of the Sierra Nevada range, twelve miles from my old homestead in Weimar. My memories are not from within the place itself, but from the people it holds. Here lie generations of family. Mama went to her rest at the age of ninety-two. Her final resting place was with Daddy. Milton's and Millie's graves are nearby, as well as those of many other family members. It helps me realize how delicate life is, as I ponder how it has taken people I loved before I expected them to go. It helps me to grasp how their breath of life left their earthly bodies and peacefully moved them into the heart of Jesus.

As I'm writing this, I'm looking at family pictures of the last time I visited the wide-open space. I recall how, in air fragrant with the scent of pine needles, we laid floral tributes of red, yellow, and pink roses. The sky suddenly filled with the most brilliant amber, complemented perfectly with hues of amethyst and pink. Sunset is merely a prelude to the dawn, yet its majesty filled our hearts as we held hands and sang the last verse of "Beyond the Sunset":

> Beyond the sunset,
> O glad reunion,
> With our dear loved ones
> Who've gone before;
> In that fair homeland
> We'll know no parting,
> Beyond the sunset
> For evermore![1]

Beyond Ashes

Jesus is the Master Creator of nature and music. In that brief window of time, we felt the love. We were not alone; we had memories tucked in our hearts. My eyes drifted upward in oneness with the glow in the sky. Like the sunset, what a glorious place this will be when Jesus comes! The graves will be opened, and loved ones will rise to be forever together in heaven and in our earth made new. Sequin-silver stars, like sparkling diamonds, winked down, illuminating the sky. The clouds rolled apart, and I found myself looking at the lustrous rays of moonlight brightening the grounds.

Yes, I am blessed that I had Mama and Daddy for parents. What a legacy they left! As we stood there in the light of the celestial sky, we reminisced how in his teen years, Daddy, like David the psalmist, had helped support his family by working as a shepherd boy. Sheep are vulnerable to danger from mountain lions and other predators because they cannot run very fast, and they are not always smart enough to avoid peril. Daddy's job was to care for the flock, keeping them safe, nourished, and happy. He reminisced that many times during the day a sheep would leave the flock and trot over to him. He would tenderly caress the sheep's head, whispering calming endearments in its ear. Encouraged and reassured, the sheep would go back to graze with the rest of the flock. Like those sheep, we need daily affirmation and reassurance from God. In confidence we can know He will give us time to catch our breath and will guide us into a path of right living.

If I could summarize what I have written in this book, it would be: "Jesus loves me; this I know."

---

1. Virgil P. Brock, "Beyond the Sunset" (n.p.: Rodeheaver, 1964), Hymnlyrics.org, accessed February 26, 2018, https://www.hymnlyrics.org/newlyrics_b/beyond_the_sunset_o_blissful_morning.php.